What peo

Empowering Climate Action in the United States

We urgently need public engagement on the climate issue, and this book couldn't be more timely.
Jeff Nesbit, Executive Director, Climate Nexus

Tackling the climate crisis offers enormous opportunities to advance health, well-being, equity, and security — to create better lives and deliver a better future for all. Embracing this potential requires widespread information-sharing and public engagement. The ACE Strategic Planning Framework is a readable, inspiring trail map for that journey. Read it, sign on to it, act on it!
Howard Frumkin, Former Director, National Center for Environmental Health, US Centers for Disease Control and Prevention

The UNFCCC Article 6 Action for Climate Empowerment agenda plays a crucial role in directing humanity to respond to the climate crisis. Recognizing this, a group of leaders from a wide range of disciplines and communities has built a strategic planning framework for the United States. This is an urgently needed effort. I urge policymakers to embrace this framework for engaging and empowering the public to act on climate.
Michael Mann, Distinguished Professor, Penn State University and Author of *The New Climate War: The Fight to Take Back Our Planet*

Creating space for real conversations is challenging, but it's the best way to solve problems together. The ACE process is like a road map, and the results are truly inspiring.

Heidi Harmon, Mayor, City of San Luis Obispo, California

In shaping this smart climate agenda that empowers all Americans, Tom Bowman, Deb Morrison, and a large group of diverse leaders have done something remarkable. At just the right moment for a nation recovering from a devastating pandemic shock and years of political toxicity, they have identified a modest passage in the global climate agreement that the new presidential administration can grasp to vault back into global leadership. Their efforts will create opportunities for all citizens to find a place in a grand effort building equitable resilience and an energy system that works for the long haul.

Andrew Revkin, climate journalist since 1985 and founding director of Columbia University's Earth Institute Initiative on Communication and Sustainability

Solving the climate crisis will require the coordinated actions not just of 190+ national leaders, but the coordinated actions of 7.5 billion human beings worldwide. It is essential to inform, engage, and empower all people to understand the risks of intensifying climate change, to prepare for the impacts, and to build the safer, healthier, more equitable, and prosperous world we and our children want to live in. This short book outlines a framework by which the United States can again lead the world by developing and implementing the first national strategy to empower the American people, in partnership with government, business, and civil society, to protect the life-support systems of our shared planet, rebuild our nation, and set an example for the world to follow.

Anthony Leiserowitz, Director, Yale Program on Climate Change Communication

The ACE National Strategy Planning Framework makes it clear that an engaged, climate-literate public can be the United States' greatest asset in climate action, and a special brand of global climate leadership. This framework is built on the best of cross-sector thinking and engagement and reinforced by climate and social sciences. It recommends the first and best path forward as a nation: by and for The People.
Sarah Sutton, Cultural Sector Lead, We Are Still In

The Action for Climate Empowerment National Strategic Planning Framework offers a toolkit for groups hoping to create their own roadmaps, drawing together the wisdom found throughout our society, including the academic community.
Baruch Fischhoff, Howard Heinz Professor, Institute for Policy and Strategy, Carnegie Mellon University

The science is unequivocal: humans are causing our world to warm. The need for large-scale action to avoid the worst scenarios grows ever more urgent. Now we have a new Action for Climate Empowerment National Strategic Planning Framework to point the way forward. The next step is clear: develop and implement an ACE strategic plan and, thus, restore US climate leadership among the international community.
David Herring, Communication, Education, and Engagement Division Chief, NOAA Climate Program Office

Previous Books by Tom Bowman

Resetting Our Future: What if Solving the Climate Crisis Is Simple?

ISBN: 978 1 78904 747 9

ISBN: 978 1 78904 748 6

The Green Edge

ISBN: 978 0 99157 030 0

Previous Books by Deb Morrison, Editor

Critical Race Spatial Analysis: Mapping to Understand and Address Educational Inequity

ISBN: 978 1 62036 423 9

ISBN: 978 1 62036 424 6

ISBN: 978 1 62036 426 0

RESETTING OUR FUTURE

Empowering Climate Action in the United States

Resetting Our Future

Empowering Climate Action in the United States

Tom Bowman and Deb Morrison

Editors

CHANGEMAKERS
BOOKS

Winchester, UK
Washington, USA

JOHN HUNT PUBLISHING

First published by Changemakers Books, 2021
Changemakers Books is an imprint of John Hunt Publishing Ltd., No. 3 East Street,
Alresford, Hampshire SO24 9EE, UK
office@jhpbooks.com
www.johnhuntpublishing.com
www.changemakers-books.com

For distributor details and how to order please visit the 'Ordering' section on our website.

Text copyright: Tom Bowman and Deb Morrison 2020

ISBN: 978 1 78904 872 8
978 1 78904 873 5 (ebook)
Library of Congress Control Number: 2020945769

A CIP catalogue record for this book is available from the British Library.

Design: Stuart Davies

UK: Printed and bound by CPI Group (UK) Ltd, Croydon, CR0 4YY
Printed in North America by CPI GPS partners

We operate a distinctive and ethical publishing philosophy in
all areas of our business, from our global network of authors to
production and worldwide distribution.

Contents

The *Resetting Our Future* Series

At this critical moment of history, with a pandemic raging, we have the rare opportunity for a Great Reset – to choose a different future. This series provides a platform for pragmatic thought leaders to share their vision for change based on their deep expertise. For communities and nations struggling to cope with the crisis, these books will provide a burst of hope and energy to help us take the first difficult steps towards a better future.
– Tim Ward, publisher, Changemakers Books

What if Solving the Climate Crisis Is Simple?
Tom Bowman, President of Bowman Change, Inc., and writing-team lead for the U.S. ACE National Strategic Planning Framework

Zero Waste Living, the 80/20 Way
The Busy Person's Guide to a Lighter Footprint
Stephanie Miller, Founder of Zero Waste in DC, and former Director, IFC Climate Business Department.

A Chicken Can't Lay a Duck Egg
How COVID-19 can Solve the Climate Crisis
Graeme Maxton, (former Secretary-General of the Club of Rome), and Bernice Maxton-Lee (former Director, Jane Goodall Institute)

A Global Playbook for the Next Pandemic
Anne Kabagambe, former World Bank Executive Director

Power Switch
How We Can Reverse Extreme Inequality
Paul O'Brien, VP Policy and Advocacy, Oxfam America

Impact ED
How Community College Entrepreneurship Creates Equity and Prosperity
Rebecca Corbin (President & CEO, National Association of Community College Entrepreneurship), Andrew Gold and Mary Beth Kerly (both business faculty, Hillsborough Community College)

Empowering Public Climate Action in the United States
Tom Bowman (President of Bowman Change, Inc.) and Deb Morrison (Learning Scientist, University of Washington)

Learning from Tomorrow
Using Strategic Foresight to Prepare for the Next Big Disruption
Bart Édes, former North American Representative, Asian Development Bank

Provocateurs not Philanthropists
Turning Good Intentions into Global Impact
Maiden R. Manzanal-Frank, Strategy Maven at GlobalStakes Consulting

SMART Futures for a Flourishing World
A Paradigm Shift for Achieving the Sustainable Development Goals
Dr. Claire Nelson, Chief Visionary Officer and Lead Futurist, The Futures Forum

Cut Super Climate Pollutants, Now!
The Ozone Treaty's Urgent Lessons for Speeding Up Climate Action
Alan Miller (former World Bank representative for global climate negotiations) and Durwood Zaelke, (President, The Institute for Governance & Sustainable Development, and co-director, The Program on Governance for Sustainable

Development at UC Santa Barbara)

Lead Different

Designing a Post-COVID Paradigm for Thriving at Work and at Home

Monica Brand, Lisa Neuberger & Wendy Teleki

Reconstructing Blackness

Rev. Charles Howard, Chaplin, University of Pennsylvania, Philadelphia

www.ResettingOurFuture.com

For those who work to empower humanity — now and throughout history — to overcome the climate crisis and systemic racism around the world, and to those who supported this remarkable project

Preface

This book contains a stand-alone report, *An ACE National Strategic Planning Framework for the United States.* That report is the collective product of 150 individuals who work on climate action and public empowerment. We wrote the report to organize and summarize their contributions. We put this book together to provide additional context and explanations, and to clarify what made the *Strategic Planning Framework* initiative so successful. We are the authors of the first three chapters and the last. The writers of the commentaries speak for themselves. In our view, they help express the breadth of this effort, as well as the potential that a national strategy for public participation will have in accelerating climate action.

The benefits of creating a national strategy are many. For the first time, initiatives by governments, philanthropists, community-based organizations, businesses, social scientists, climate scientists, social marketers, health communicators, and many others, can be aligned to maximize their collective impact. ACE work in the United States has been multi-faceted and highly skilled for many years. Creating a national strategy will direct funding to places where it can do the most good, optimize outreach to a remarkably diverse range of audiences, build capacity in local communities, guide policy development, and much more.

ACE, or Action for Climate Empowerment, is part of the United Nations Framework Convention on Climate Change and the historic Paris Agreement. We are confident that this book can help the United States and a much larger community of nations find common purpose in responding to the climate crisis. This book is written for them, and for anyone who cares deeply about the future and would be buoyed by a realistic expression of hope.

Foreword

by Thomas Lovejoy

The pandemic has changed our world. Lives have been lost. Livelihoods as well. Far too many face urgent problems of health and economic security, but almost all of us are reinventing our lives in one way or another. Meeting the immediate needs of the less fortunate is obviously a priority, and a big one. But beyond those compassionate imperatives, there is also tremendous opportunity for what some people are calling a "Great Reset." This series of books, *Resetting Our Future*, is designed to provide pragmatic visionary ideas and stimulate a fundamental rethink of the future of humanity, nature and the economy.

I find myself thinking about my parents, who had lived through the Second World War and the Great Depression, and am still impressed by the sense of frugality they had attained. When packages arrived in the mail, my father would save the paper and string; he did it so systematically I don't recall our ever having to buy string. Our diets were more careful: whether it could be afforded or not, beef was restricted to once a week. When aluminum foil—the great boon to the kitchen—appeared, we used and washed it repeatedly until it fell apart. Bottles, whether Coca-Cola or milk, were recycled.

Waste was consciously avoided. My childhood task was to put out the trash; what goes out of my backdoor today is an unnecessary multiple of that. At least some of it now goes to recycling but a lot more should surely be possible.

There was also a widespread sense of service to a larger community. Military service was required of all. But there was also the Civilian Conservation Corps, which had provided jobs and repaired the ecological destruction that had generated the Dust Bowl. The Kennedy administration introduced the Peace

Corps and the President's phrase "Ask not what your country can do for you but what you can do for your country" still resonates in our minds.

There had been antecedents, but in the 1970s there was a global awakening about a growing environmental crisis. In 1972, The United Nations held its first conference on the environment at Stockholm. Most of the modern US institutions and laws about environment were established under moderate Republican administrations (Nixon and Ford). Environment was seen not just as appealing to "greenies" but also as a thoughtful conservative's issue. The largest meeting of Heads of State in history, the Earth Summit, took place in Rio de Janeiro in 1992 and three international conventions—climate change, biodiversity (on which I was consulted) and desertification— came into existence.

But three things changed. First, there now are three times as many people alive today as when I was born and each new person deserves a minimum quality of life. Second, the sense of frugality was succeeded by a growing appetite for affluence and an overall attitude of entitlement. And third, conservative political advisors found advantage in demonizing the environment as comity vanished from the political dialogue.

Insufficient progress has brought humanity and the environment to a crisis state. The CO_2 level in the atmosphere at 415 ppm (parts per million) is way beyond a non-disruptive level around 350 ppm. (The pre-industrial level was 280 ppm.)

Human impacts on nature and biodiversity are not just confined to climate change. Those impacts will not produce just a long slide of continuous degradation. The pandemic is a direct result of intrusion upon, and destruction of, nature as well as wild-animal trade and markets. The scientific body of the UN Convention on Biological Diversity warned in 2020 that we could lose a million species unless there are major changes in human interactions with nature.

We still can turn those situations around. Ecosystem restoration at scale could pull carbon back out of the atmosphere for a soft landing at 1.5 degrees of warming (at 350 ppm), hand in hand with a rapid halt in production and use of fossil fuels. The Amazon tipping point where its hydrological cycle would fail to provide enough rain to maintain the forest in southern and eastern Amazonia can be solved with major reforestation. The oceans' biology is struggling with increasing acidity, warming and ubiquitous pollution with plastics: addressing climate change can lower the first two and efforts to remove plastics from our waste stream can improve the latter.

Indisputably, we need a major reset in our economies, what we produce, and what we consume. We exist on an amazing living planet, with a biological profusion that can provide humanity a cornucopia of benefits—and more that science has yet to reveal—and all of it is automatically recyclable because nature is very good at that. Scientists have determined that we can, in fact, feed all the people on the planet, and the couple billion more who may come, by a combination of selective improvements of productivity, eliminating food waste and altering our diets (which our doctors have been advising us to do anyway).

The *Resetting Our Future* series is intended to help people think about various ways of economic and social rebuilding that will support humanity for the long term. There is no single way to do this and there is plenty of room for creativity in the process, but nature with its capacity for recovery and for recycling can provide us with much inspiration, including ways beyond our current ability to imagine.

Ecosystems do recover from shocks, but the bigger the shock, the more complicated recovery can be. At the end of the Cretaceous period (66 million years ago) a gigantic meteor slammed into the Caribbean near the Yucatan and threw up so much dust and debris into the atmosphere that much of biodiversity perished. It was *sayonara* for the dinosaurs; their only surviving close relatives were precursors to modern day birds. It certainly was not a good time for life on Earth.

The clear lesson of the pandemic is that it makes no sense to generate a global crisis and then hope for a miracle. We are lucky to have the pandemic help us reset our relation to the Living Planet as a whole. We already have building blocks like the United Nations Sustainable Development Goals and various environmental conventions to help us think through more effective goals and targets. The imperative is to rebuild with humility and imagination, while always conscious of the health of the living planet on which we have the joy and privilege to exist.

Dr. Thomas E. Lovejoy is Professor of Environmental Science and Policy at George Mason University and a Senior Fellow at the United Nations Foundation. A world-renowned conservation biologist, Dr. Lovejoy introduced the term "biological diversity" to the scientific community.

Chapter 1

Welcome to the Strategic Planning Framework

We have the privilege of introducing you to something extraordinary. The United States has been given an unprecedented opportunity to make an inspired recovery from the traumas of 2020. Amid the tragedy of a deadly pandemic, a profound economic crisis, an awakening to systemic racism and violence against Black, Indigenous, and People of Color (BIPOC), and a divisive national election, a professionally and demographically diverse group of people came together, voluntarily, to guide the federal government and other stakeholders in developing a novel response to the climate crisis.

For decades, talented, highly skilled people and organizations have worked to help the public in the United States understand climate change and environmental injustice and participate in finding and implementing solutions. Their efforts have been impressive, yet diffused and fragmented. Lacking the guidance that a coherent overall strategy would provide, they have shown creative ingenuity and entrepreneurial initiative, yet they have struggled against significant barriers in their efforts to achieve the scale of collective impact that humanity urgently needs.

In 2020, members of this diverse group of people took a risk. They chose to collaborate as equals in co-developing a unifying strategic planning framework in order to build and test the infrastructure for creating a national strategic plan. Their mission was firmly grounded in the global climate treaty known as the United Nations Framework Convention on Climate Change (UNFCCC) and its offspring, the historic Paris Agreement. UNFCCC Article 6 lays out the Action for Climate

Empowerment (ACE) goals and urges all signatory nations to embrace them. Article 12 of the Paris Agreement reaffirms this recommendation and its importance.[1]

Through ACE, the community of nations affirms that activating people as co-creators of new policies, understandings, and behavioral norms is the fastest and most efficient way to accelerate a transition to a low-carbon world that is equitable and just. As we write these words, however, no major emitting country has submitted a national strategy for ACE to the UNFCCC. This includes the United States. With *An ACE National Strategic Planning Framework for the United States* (*Strategic Planning Framework*), the processes that created it, and subsequent efforts to encourage its adoption by government decision-makers, private philanthropists, and others, the community of ACE actors in the U.S. seeks to change this reality.

The *Strategic Planning Framework*'s focus on co-creation, meaningful community-level participation, equity, and empowerment makes it unique among all of the strategic approaches that have been developed by other nations thus far. If the U.S. creates an ACE national strategy as recommended in these pages, the country will make groundbreaking contributions to the global fight against climate change. In addition to motivating the public in the United States, it will offer a model that other nations can follow in activating humanity's capacity to address the common threats to our shared future.

We are the writers of the *Strategic Planning Framework*, but not its authors. The document is actually the collaborative product of the 150 people who conceived and coordinated the initiative and contributed the content, the 20 strategic reviewers who tuned an early draft, and the ACE community members who provided the final review. As the commentaries in this book will show, the people who know the ACE landscape best—from many different perspectives—are the real authors of the *Strategic Planning Framework* and the crucial decisions that led to its creation.

Who Owns the Climate Issue?

For decades, the people and organizations that work on various aspects of the ACE agenda have done so within different professional silos: climate science, behavioral science, education, strategic communication, journalism, climate and environmental justice, policymaking, civil service, philanthropy, business, finance, health, international aid and development, activism, the arts, law, and a host of others. Each silo has its own mission, professional culture, rewards systems, and limitations. Each makes important contributions to public understanding and the capacity for action, yet none can create an engaged and empowered society on its own.

From a historical perspective, it is safe to say that climate scientists and politicians have dominated the nation's framing and responses to the climate issue. Scientists and science educators have sought to increase people's knowledge and understanding of the scientific evidence and the risks we face. Politicians, for their part, have applied various ideological and philosophical lenses to the issue and preached diverging interpretations to their supporters. Political competition over the climate issue has also provided an opening and support for the well-funded and strategic disinformation campaigns led by fossil fuel interests and ideological libertarians to mislead the public, undermine confidence in the settled science, and dissuade people from taking action to reduce global warming.[2]

The public's sense of ownership of the climate crisis has shifted in recent years. In 2020, public concern had reached an all-time high that was driven, at least in part, by a confluence of factors: public statements by trusted sources other than climate scientists such as doctors, health organizations, and television meteorologists; people's first-hand experiences of the changing environment in the communities where they live; and the rise of overlapping and very public climate justice movements led by BIPOC (Black, Indigenous, and People of Color) and youth.

8

The *Strategic Planning Framework* rejects the proposition that any single profession, influential group, or geographical community owns the issue at all. Climate change is everyone's crisis and it is everyone's crisis to solve. As one co-creator put it, "The bad news is that there is a lot of work to do. The good news is that there is plenty of work for everyone."[3] The ACE agenda, in fact, affirms that everyone has the right and the obligation to determine what the future will be. As the *Resetting Our Future* book series points out, the future is humanity's to collectively reset.

Consider, for a moment, how you would go about creating a unifying ACE strategic plan for so many different types of ACE actors in such a diverse society. One suggestion was that strategic planning could be assigned to a federal agency or a multi-agency task force, presumably in collaboration with a consulting firm. The cost of such an effort would certainly be high. In contrast, organizing an unsanctioned, voluntary, grassroots process by the ACE community itself seemed risky, if not impossible.

The organizers of *Strategic Planning Framework* initiative rejected these views. They knew that a top-down, agency-led process—with the agency's inherent biases and obligations—would be too narrow and, potentially, irrelevant to many of the people who do so much of the nation's ACE work. Given that submitting an ACE national strategy to the UNFCCC is, by definition, an official act of the United States, however, government involvement was essential. The influence of a unified national strategy on ACE investments, guidelines, and policies, moreover, made government involvement extremely beneficial. Yet an effective national strategy also demands a multi-faceted, multi-sectoral approach that is informed by a wider range of experiences and expertise than government agencies, alone, can provide. *An ACE National Strategic Planning Framework for the United States*, therefore, was developed by people from both inside and outside of government who have strong commitments and deep experience in many facets of this agenda.

Welcoming Diversity and Embracing Equity

In his book, *The Magic of Dialogue*, social scientist Daniel Yankelovich describes a particular type of conversation that is designed to build mutual understanding and trust. This type of dialogue requires participants to leave their roles, organizational logos, social stature, and power relationships at the door. The goal is not to negotiate a settlement, but rather to learn everyone's perspectives, appreciate everyone's concerns, and recognize the expertise and wisdom that everyone brings to a shared challenge. As noted in the *Strategic Planning Framework*, Yankelovich writes:

> In traditional hierarchical arrangements, those at the top of the pecking order can afford to be casual about how well they understand those at lower levels. When people are more equal, they are obligated to make a greater effort to understand each other. If no one is the undisputed boss anymore, and if all insist on having their views respected, it follows that people must understand each other. You don't really have a voice if those making the decisions aren't prepared to listen to you.[4]

"A dialogue among equals" defined the *Strategic Planning Framework* process. Those who participated in this initiative adopted the U.N.'s Talanoa Dialogue Platform,[5] which is a Fijian approach to decision-making that embraces a very similar process and understanding. In the Talanoa process, everyone participates as a decision-maker. Dialogues do not merely provide input to the powers that be; they are the process in which wise decisions are made by and for a community.

The definition of "equals" is also important. The organizers of this initiative were pressed to ensure that historically marginalized people were equal participants in every aspect of planning, dialogue, writing, and review. The results were transformational for those who participated. As one Caucasian participant noted privately:

> I said that marginalized groups are OUR natural allies. Who did I mean by "our?"...It places BIPOC outside whoever is included in "our." I think I meant liberal climate change activists aligned with the big green groups, but is there a presumption of whiteness there?...I make the presumption of whiteness as the norm, which makes BIPOC outsiders. I will try to be more careful in future about my use of language here.[6]

Many of us found that the dialogues challenged our sense that "we" somehow own the climate crisis and its solutions, that our perspectives should be normative, that our knowledge is somehow preferred, and that we can retain decision-making authority while also "being inclusive" of others. Talanoa-style dialogues help people break free of these narrow and destructive assumptions. Many of us found the dialogues to be deeply inspiring yet somewhat uncomfortable when they disrupted our familiar, if misleading, sense of identity as "leading" or "authoritative" ACE actors. We learned, instead, that our biases are critical barriers to generating active public participation and the collective impact that society needs. We learned, in other words, how engaging with others as equal co-creators—rather than asserting our familiar power relationships—exposes the depth of knowledge, wisdom, and capacity that already exists throughout society.

Knowledge, wisdom, and capacity are intrinsic to people everywhere. If you, too, feel challenged by some of what you read in the *Strategic Planning Framework*, we hope that you will keep an open mind and feel hopeful about what a national strategy for public empowerment can accomplish on everyone's behalf. This would be a good outcome because diversity is likely to be humanity's greatest asset in an economic recovery that leads to a more just, equitable, and low-carbon world.

We hasten to stress, moreover, that collaboration depends upon building lasting relationships and mutual trust among people, organizations, and networks. Working on ACE is a long-term investment. Many people are accustomed to collaborating on a product or a one-off event. In the context of the *Strategic Planning Framework*, however, we need to leverage the productive, long-standing relationships that already exist and foster new long-term relationships that will promote trust and ongoing co-creation of an increasingly just and equitable low-carbon future.

In the chapters and commentaries that follow, and in the *Strategic Planning Framework* itself, you will discover what a national strategy for a diverse society could look like. Keep in mind that diversity and equity should not be limited only to those who co-created the *Strategic Framework* that you are about to read. This was a pilot project. Those who participated did so voluntarily, largely because they trusted other participants whom they knew. These were people who are actively engaged in the climate issue in one capacity or another, and the *Strategic Framework* reflects their commitments.

The *Strategic Planning Framework* strongly recommends that the dialogue process must be extended further to include others who will have additional insights, wisdom, professional expertise, and lived experience to contribute. Future dialogues might include additional members of rural communities, businesses, faith communities, the science community, the public health community, and others. The *Strategic Planning Framework* explicitly points out the need to provide financial support for BIPOC participants and those in poverty, as these communities are often already working at the limits of their capacity to participate in solving the climate crisis. An equally strong case can be made for supporting members of rural communities, the owners of small businesses, and others whose participation would be limited in the absence of financial support. The goal of a national strategy for ACE is to speak for the nation, not merely for those who have the privilege and means to represent themselves.

The *Strategic Planning Framework* provides a case study in the infrastructure for developing a national strategy: a shared vision, specific recommendations, and a procedural roadmap. The commentaries in this book express what a national strategy will mean and what it can help us achieve. At its core, the *Strategic Planning Framework*, and the ACE agenda itself, help shift our focus from technocratic carbon accounting to the lives of the people whose behaviors and choices will determine what the world becomes in the next few decades. The best way to ensure a vibrant and resilient future is to increase people's capacity to be its co-creators.

Chapter 2

Discoveries and Assumptions

Bringing together a diverse community of educators, advocates, communication specialists, and others to engage in collaborative development of a *Strategic Planning Framework* allowed us to appreciate the incredible people, communities, and organizations engaged in climate action across the United States. As writers, we had the added benefit of listening to all of the dialogues and reading every note that was taken and review that was provided. This access allowed us to discover a few underlying assumptions that were widely shared by the ACE community members who contributed. While these assumptions are demonstrated throughout the *Strategic Planning Framework* in various ways, articulating them more explicitly will help orient you to what the community has said. Those who will carry the ACE community's work forward will also benefit from a clear understanding of why certain attributes of ACE are so central to the community's vision and recommendations. The following assumptions emerged from the ACE *Strategic Planning Framework* conversations:

1. *The ACE community accepts the conclusions of the science community that human-caused climate change is occurring.* We witnessed no false debate about the validity of the scientific evidence or doubt about the extraordinarily high level of scientific consensus. Many of the dialogue participants, in fact, described some of the ways in which the changing climate is already impacting the communities they serve. We hasten to note, however, that confidence in the scientific consensus on climate change is not universally shared by the public. Whereas 73 percent of Americans think "global warming is happening,"

62 percent understand that it is "mostly human-caused," and 54 percent understand that most scientists "think global warming is happening," "Only about one in five (21 percent) understand how strong the level of consensus among scientists is (i.e., that more than 90 percent of climate scientists think human-caused global warming is happening.)"[1] A national strategy for ACE and the processes through which a wider group of stakeholders are invited into the dialogue process must be responsive to these realities about public understanding and public opinion.

2. *The ACE community accepts the fundamental premise of the UNFCCC ACE goals*, which is that people must be informed and empowered participants in creating their own future. The ACE community in the United States goes somewhat further by saying, in effect, that a successful response to the climate challenge literally depends upon widespread public participation in finding and implementing solutions. Dialogue participants do not believe that a top-down approach will be sufficient. They assert, with great confidence, that individuals and local communities — everywhere — possess tremendous knowledge, wisdom, creativity, and a capacity for collective action that the nation and all of humanity need. The *Strategic Planning Framework* notes, for example, that federal agencies have been among the actors that have improved the public's understanding and capacity to make informed choices, yet federal political leadership has been marked by turmoil, equivocation, and compromise.

3. *In a society that is as diverse and dispersed as that of the United States, people will inevitably have different policy preferences.* Such differences were evident in the dialogues, and some of them appear in the *Strategic Planning Framework* as illustrative examples of the co-creators' assembled inputs and convictions. The *Strategic Planning Framework* itself does not take policy

positions. It asserts, instead, that people should be empowered to participate in co-creating and implementing an ACE national strategy and climate-related policies. If everyone faces climate risks, then everyone has a right to participate in finding solutions.

These latter two points deserve further discussion.

The Central Roles of Equity and Justice

The *Strategic Planning Framework* and the guidelines provided by the United Nations Educational, Scientific, and Cultural Organization (UNESCO) and the UNFCCC Secretariat, which informed the development process, assert that empowering the public will accelerate a just transition to a low-carbon future. You will discover, in fact, that climate solutions and climate justice are described as inseparable from one another. Furthermore, the ACE community asserts that inequitable, unjust decision-making processes can only lead to unjust outcomes.

If these statements strike you as unusual—even groundbreaking—in a discussion about climate change, it is with good reason. Climate solutions have long been discussed, by and large, in relatively abstract, technocratic language. High-level policymaking has been focused on regulatory, financial, and incentive mechanisms that will promote the transition from a fossil energy economy to a "clean," "green," or "renewable" economy, often through top-down approaches. Justice, on the other hand, is often described as a moral ideal that the nation strives, yet fails, to achieve. Inside the nation's governing and power infrastructure, climate justice and the wellbeing of people who live in low-income and BIPOC communities are often treated like moral goals that are, sadly, impossible to fully achieve. Equity and climate justice look entirely different in the communities that are disadvantaged most by the impacts of climate change, and where people have the fewest resources to increase their own resilience. In low-income and BIPOC communities, equity and justice are practical matters.

The ACE agenda calls for a shift in governance in ways that may be challenging to those who are accustomed to exercising power and authority. The UNESCO/UNFCCC Secretariat ACE guidelines state:

> By ensuring that people can participate effectively in climate change decision-making and implement climate mitigation and adaptation activities, governments should seek to integrate civil society perspectives and mobilize the general public. In some places this will prompt profound changes in how political leaders and civil servants are accustomed to working and encourage people to be more attentive to policy-making.[2]

In some countries, seeking input from the public will challenge existing governing structures and power relationships. In the United States, where people freely express their opinions and can engage with political leaders, it means going beyond seeking opinions. The case for genuine public empowerment and participation hinges on building relationships with the people who can co-create the transition to a low-carbon future. We witnessed this process take shape in the Talanoa-style dialogues and throughout the writing and review process, and the experience was transformational.

Entering into meaningful collaboration with a diverse community of people requires that everyone reconsider who possesses power and how that power has been used. Working in relationship with others means that the processes by which an ACE strategic plan is created need to ensure equitable participation and provide the financial resources that will enable low-income community members to participate fully and as equals. Historic grievances and structural inequities in who can exercise power need to be resolved.

If this reads like a progressive political agenda, consider this:

the need to resolve historic inequities, as well as the injustices that they lead to, is an inevitable consequence of the climate crisis. The changing climate is of urgent concern to everyone and every ecosystem on this planet. Reducing global warming and creating greater climate resilience will require all hands to be engaged and everyone's knowledge to be shared. Lasting solutions will require local expertise and local implementation.

But local knowledge and expertise are not resources that belong to the political establishment. Attempting to mine them from local communities for the sake of others is both unjust and impractical. Those who hold such knowledge and expertise—especially BIPOC—are under no obligation to share what they know with anyone else. Such sharing depends upon trust and genuinely reciprocal collaboration. "Reciprocal" does not mean transactional; it is a description of human nature. It means participating in respectful relationships where all parties come to understand and respect one another and share to whatever degree their level of trust allows. There can be no universal participation in solving the climate crisis unless people are willing to resolve long-standing grievances and create genuine pathways for sharing power with one another.

We acknowledge that the recommendations expressed in the *Strategic Planning Framework* might appear challenging to some readers while being a breath of fresh air to others. These views have intrinsic merit and validity, and they should not be undermined in any way. Keep in mind that creating a truly national strategic plan for public engagement and empowerment will also require dialogues in which people who hold different values, commitments, and practical concerns will participate. Their recommendations will also have standing. The dialogue process is designed to be inclusive, cut across familiar silos, capture the full range of recommendations, and build strategies that speak to the welfare of our collective society. In chapter three, we offer some thoughts about how this remarkable pilot project can be expanded to include members of rural communities, the diverse range of faith and wisdom communities, and the business community, among others.

Understanding a Few Key Terms

An ACE National Strategic Planning Framework for the United States uses a number of terms in the context of equity and justice that might be unclear to those of you who have not been immersed in such dialogues. In simple terms, we understand them as follows.

1. *"BIPOC"* came to prominence in 2020 as a way to differentiate and also identify common experiences among Black, Indigenous, and other People of Color in relation to anti-Blackness and systemic racism. Although the meaning of this short acronym seems self-evident, the term vastly oversimplifies the diverse experiences of people living in every part of the United States. Such experiences are often overlapping. For example, Indigenous people face racism, linguistic and cultural eradication, limitations on the right of self-determination including the failure to honor treaties, dispossession of lands, and exploitation of culture. Black people face racism rooted in official policies of exclusion and dehumanization, historic and ongoing violence that is both physical and mental, and limitations on their opportunities based both in attitudes and law. More generally, People of Color experience racism in ways that are overlapping with their own linguistic, ethnic, religious, and national origins. As writers, we attempted to provide context when using "BIPOC," but we understand that the term evokes meanings that are inherently complex and multi-dimensional.

2. *"Diversity"* is used throughout the *Strategic Planning Framework*, but without a specific definition. This is by design. The word "diversity" often conjures the impression that people

of different ethnic groups, religious backgrounds, nationalities, ages, abilities, genders, gender identities, and other factors will be represented in various proportions to one another. While equitable representation is important, "representational diversity," alone, actually fails to capture the deeper meaning of the term. As the *Strategic Planning Framework* states, "The U.S. ACE Agenda: Recognizes and builds upon the diversity of knowledge, expertise, values, and ways of knowing and acting throughout society."[3] This statement acknowledges that our familiar labels for groups of people give a false impression that they are monolithic. As noted in the discussion of "BIPOC," above, people in different circumstances—for example, urban, suburban, rural, affluence, poverty—have different overlapping and intersective concerns, experiences, knowledge, expertise, values, and so on. While categories of race, religion, gender, gender identity, age, education, ability, and other characteristics are social constructs that have real-world consequences, true inclusion requires that we think beyond stereotypical and superficial labels to really learn from—and collaborate on—climate action together.

3. *"Inclusion"* is a term that is used to describe who can exercise power. "Inclusion" sounds welcoming to many Caucasians, but it is synonymous with "assimilation" to the BIPOC co-creators of the *Strategic Planning Framework*. One contributor said that "inclusion" means "you have a seat at the table, but you can't order from the menu."[4] In other words, those who hold power might solicit your input, but they have no intention of sharing their decision-making authority with you. Understanding this, we avoided using "inclusion" and "inclusive" in the *Strategic Planning Framework*. We encourage everyone who works on ACE to be thoughtful about what these terms mean to other people and about the need to disrupt and restructure the power relationships that these terms imply.

4. *"America"* seems simple enough. It refers to the United States. We talk about "the American people," and sing *America the Beautiful*. Yet the ACE agenda is part of an international treaty, and the U.S. ACE national strategy will represent the country around the world. Co-creators who have international experience, especially with IPCC processes, pointed out that, in the context of ACE at least, "American" refers equally to all of the countries in North, Central, and South America. We learned that other countries resent the appropriation of this name by the United States in the context of the UNFCCC. As a result, we avoid saying "America" and "American" in the *Strategic Planning Framework*.

5. *"Governments"* is commonly understood to refer to nations, and many people assume that a national government speaks for an entire nation. Indeed, international cooperation and collaboration is a central pillar of how ACE is formulated, so understanding what "governments" means is extremely important. The *Strategic Planning Framework* was developed with a clear recognition that the United States is not a monolithic entity, and that decisions are not made by a single "government." As writers, we attempted to make clear that the term "governments" refers to the complex and overlapping jurisdictions and relationships between Federal, Tribal, State, and local authorities.

6. *"Rural"* is another term that sounds simple but is actually complex. In popular media, "rural" often means white communities with farming, mining, or forestry economies. You might think of people who live in rural communities as having fairly conservative political perspectives and Christian religious affiliations. This stereotype of "rural America" oversimplifies the diversity of rural populations and regions across the United States. For example, large numbers of BIPOC live outside of cities and suburbs. BIPOC and white rural people hold diverse

viewpoints, political stances, and faith commitments. One commonality among all of these rural peoples is the increased vulnerability that their close proximity to nature and their relative lack of resources brings. Rural people often live in close relationships to the natural ecosystems and are thus keenly aware of and personally knowledgeable about the emerging impacts of climate change. Many rural people and governments are active participants in finding and implementing climate solutions, yet they face some unique challenges such as uneven access to Internet service, diverse learning opportunities, and economic support to engage in professional development training. The *Strategic Planning Framework* acknowledges these challenges, yet those who develop a full-fledged U.S. ACE national strategy will need to engage with diverse ACE communities in rural settings much more than we were able to do in this pilot project. We will offer some thoughts about advancing this part of the strategic planning process in the next chapter.

Finally, UNFCCC's Article 6—Action for Climate Empowerment—is part of an international treaty. As noted earlier, the treaty recognizes that implementing ACE will challenge the ways in which nations govern. In some countries, merely educating people about climate change or seeking their input and buy-in for climate-related policies will be extremely challenging. These difficulties are freely acknowledged in the treaty itself. UNFCCC processes, conferences, and documents provide guidelines, but no standards. Each nation is encouraged to develop a national strategy that is appropriate to its unique national circumstances.

ACE is also non-partisan. The co-creators' emphasis on equitable and just processes is, in reality, a reflection of the diversity of the United States and of its long-standing challenges in establishing access for everyone. We and our co-creators are well aware that such meaningful collaboration will not be part of every nation's ACE strategy, but it is necessary for the United States. Anything less will fail to build public support and meaningful participation. Such an outcome would hinder the nation's ability to achieve its climate resilience, mitigation, and equity aspirations.

The *Strategic Planning Framework* is, in fact, a precedent-setting document. This is the first time that such a diverse group of people—people with deep experience and expertise in many different aspects of ACE—have pooled their knowledge and perspectives to advise the nation on how to be more strategic, aligned, and successful in promoting public understanding and participation in order to overcome the climate challenge successfully. In the commentaries that follow later in this book, you will discover what this means to those who are dedicated to meeting that challenge.

Chapter 3

Engaging with Additional Dialogue Partners

An ACE National Strategic Planning Framework for the United States is the product of an all-volunteer pilot project. Most of the work was done with little or no financial compensation. Naturally, such a scenario attracted people who felt very strongly about climate action, climate justice, or both. It would be unrealistic to expect such a project to attract people who were less convinced that the climate crisis is real, human-caused, and dangerous, or whose financial circumstances were tenuous.

In the year 2020, the immediacy of the COVID-19 pandemic and the resulting financial crisis loomed especially large. Participants self-selected, at least in part, based on their sense of urgency about climate change and their capacity to commit whatever time and energy they chose to offer. For most people, this involved recruiting some of their peers, joining one or more multi-hour online dialogues, or reviewing one or more drafts of the *Strategic Planning Framework*. Many of the participants joined all of the dialogues and participated in the community review as well. For others, the time commitments were not especially large, yet people had to trust that their time would not be wasted. Those of us who work on climate change outreach and education have participated in more than a few well-intended collaborative exercises that built camaraderie but yielded few tangible results. Choosing to participate in this process involved a leap of faith and trust in the people who extend the invitations.

The timing of the 2020 national election helped facilitate that leap for most of the participants. After watching the Trump administration perpetuate the myth that climate science is a hoax, dismantle much of the Clean Power Plan, roll back clean air and clean water protections, open tracts of wild land to development, and prepare to leave the Paris Agreement, participants assessed that a new administration would probably be eager to demonstrate bold leadership on the climate issue.

Thus, those who co-created the *Strategic Planning Framework* were a highly experienced, knowledgeable, and motivated group of people who believed that creating an ACE national strategy would increase their collective impact and restore international leadership on behalf of the United States. They were buoyed by the prospect that a new administration might support full implementation of the Paris Agreement and embrace their work, yet they also expressed a strong belief that a joint statement by respected leaders in such a diverse ACE community would also be influential to their peers, governments, and private philanthropy organizations regardless of the outcome of the election.

It would be wrong, therefore, to say that the *Strategic Planning Framework* is the product of Democrats or the political left. It is, rather, the project of an extremely diverse community that shares similar convictions about the risks posed by the climate crisis and systemic racism, and about the benefits of informing and empowering people, organizations, and local communities to take action.

Their convictions are well founded. A 2019 report titled *Accelerating America's Climate Pledge* compiled the climate action commitments of sub-national actors across the United States. The report asserts:

An unprecedented coalition of U.S. states, cities, businesses, communities of faith, health care and cultural institutions, and other organizations are now acting to fulfill America's climate pledge to the world. This commitment is reflected in the large number of American actors continuing to back the Paris Agreement, including members of the We Are Still

In network, the U.S. Climate Alliance, Climate Mayors, We Mean Business, and many others.[1]

Together, these commitments represent well over half of the nation's economy and population:

> American coalitions of states, cities, businesses, and others committed to climate action in support of the Paris Agreement are massive and globally significant. They now represent 68 percent of U.S. GDP, 65 percent of U.S. population and 51 percent of U.S. emissions. If they were a country, these U.S. coalitions would have the world's second largest economy — second only to the United States itself.[2]

> A map of these commitments shows that they are distributed across the entire country. The concentration of commitments closely mirrors the distribution of the U.S. population across the nation's states and regions. The numbers of entities that have committed to achieving the goals of the Paris Agreement are significant as well: 25 states, 534 Tribes, 2,008 businesses, 981 faith-based and cultural organizations, 400 universities, and 38 healthcare organizations.[3]

The conclusion we draw from this distribution is that the desire for action to address the climate crisis is widespread across the country. The full breadth and depth of that commitment, however, could not be captured in a voluntary pilot project that was led by civil society, without the convening power or financial resources of the federal government, during a deadly pandemic and a deep economic crisis. Our conclusion strongly implies that the dialogue and review processes used in this pilot project were effective—even transformational—and the results are substantive and valid. An equally strong implication is that these processes should be expanded to include much wider participation by those who have not yet contributed to the development of an ACE national strategy.

As we think about engaging a wider group of stakeholders in future dialogues, it is important to remember that the dialogues were effective, to a large degree, because they brought people from disparate professional, geographical, and other "silos" together in a cross-cutting way. Conducting Talanoa-style dialogues within a single, isolated stakeholder group would not have achieved such results. The power of this process lies in the collaborative exchanges that encourage new understandings and benefit the ACE agenda as a whole.

Dialogue with Rural Communities

We have already described the complex landscape of rural communities. When we use this term we think of smaller towns and unincorporated areas with low population density, most of which feature raw material extraction, forestry, or agricultural economies. We also noted that rural communities, in general, can be multi-ethnic, multi-racial, and lower-income. Their populations often lean conservative, prefer hierarchical leadership rather than more egalitarian approaches to decision-making, and favor individual liberty and a smaller national government.[4]

On the climate issue, a majority of rural people believe that the climate is changing. There is somewhat less agreement, however, that climate change is affecting the weather and even less agreement that human activities are the cause. Awareness about the high level of scientific consensus about climate change is quite low among these populations.[5] While stewardship of the land and local ecosystems, and concerns about the welfare of local communities tend to be high priorities in rural circumstances, it is easy to understand why these populations were not strongly attracted to the *Strategic Planning Framework* pilot project. The rural participants tended to be situated in rural Indigenous communities.

Extreme poverty is also an attribute of some rural communities. A 2017 study, for example, found that a lack of basic sanitation infrastructure meant that one-third of the people tested in Lowndes County, Alabama, showed signs of the hookworm parasite. Until then, hookworm was thought to have been eradicated in the United States.[6] In California's agricultural San Joaquin Valley, an area known as "the nation's fruit and salad bowl," some 350,000 people lack access to potable water.[7] Many such regions feature relatively informal settlements on unincorporated county land, where there is little or no municipal infrastructure.

Members of such communities were not likely to join voluntary dialogues about education, training, empowerment, and participation in fighting the climate crisis. In order to participate, these people will require financial support, access to reliable high-speed Internet service, and invitations from people whom they trust. They will also need to see tangible benefits accruing from their participation. Just as Indigenous people are under no obligation to provide their knowledge and expertise to a society that has historically excluded them, neither are members of rural communities who believe that the federal government has ignored the economic and healthcare challenges they face. Genuine representation and reciprocity about issues that are tangible and meaningful will be necessary ingredients of future ACE strategic planning. Trusting relationships cannot be built otherwise.

We should also note that not all rural communities are alike, even in terms of the attributes we have just described. As more affluent people leave crowded cities to enjoy less high-pressure lifestyles closer to nature, they bring their wealth and urban attitudes with them. These demographic shifts may be disruptive to some communities. In other places, especially those with economies that feature eco-tourism, the demographic and attitudinal landscape might be significantly different.

Finally, in a rural agrarian context, the term "rural community" might or might not include migrant laborers. Whereas small towns might have relatively stable populations, these communities are, in many ways, inseparable from the large numbers of mostly-BIPOC migrant farm workers who are so important to the local economies. Migrant farm workers can be found throughout all agricultural regions of the United States, yet they stand apart from community services, decision-making, and educational systems in many ways.

As we think about expanding the *Strategic Planning Framework* pilot project, it is important to remember how diverse rural communities actually are. We need to consider what will motivate people to participate in an Action for Climate Empowerment strategic planning process, provide the necessary connectivity and financial support, and attend to the value they will expect to derive from the process. Most of all, we must find ways to bring members of these communities into dialogue with others, many of whom will come from very different circumstances and cultures.

Dialogue with Other Trusted Voices

The *Strategic Planning Framework* cites evidence from communication and social marketing researchers about the efficacy of recruiting trusted voices other than climate scientists to help inform the public about climate change. Statements made by health organizations, doctors, and broadcast meteorologists, for example, have proven to increase public confidence in climate science. Aligning and funding such efforts based on shared strategies and goals is one of the greatest benefits that an ACE national strategy has to offer.

The climate science community, itself, will benefit from greater participation in the dialogue process. Science culture is dominated by concerns over accuracy, caution, and careful delineation of the boundaries of scientific understanding. These attributes are critically important for informing the public about issues of great concern. Science alone, however, is incapable of moving the needle on the degree of public concern or commitment to collective action. The pilot project process, which emphasized multi-sectoral and multi-profession dialogues, will help foster the collaborations that are needed to better inform the public and enable people and communities to make wise decisions on their own behalf.

With this in mind, we recommend that the strategic planning process bring a variety of other trusted leaders into dialogue with scientists, activists, educators, social marketers, policymakers, civil servants, BIPOC, and others. Some of these trusted leaders might come from faith and spiritual communities, the arts, labor, and businesses. As noted above, attention must be paid to people's capacity to participate based on their financial, connectivity, and other circumstances.

In this regard, we note that none of these communities, professions, or trades is monolithic. When we think of businesses, for example, we often think of large, publicly traded corporations that operate nationally or internationally and influence national economic, health, and environmental policies. Forty-four percent of net new jobs in the U.S. and 44 percent of gross domestic product, however, are generated by smaller, local, mostly privately owned businesses.[8] These are the millions of small companies that populate every community in the nation. Unlike their larger, publicly traded peers, however, small businesses operate largely outside of policymaking processes. Their owners, by and large, lack the financial resources, influence, and free time needed to participate in political processes. The sheer number and diversity of small and medium-sized firms makes recruiting them for policymaking work especially challenging. They should not, however, be ignored, because they are situated within communities and their owners tend to be attuned to the attitudes of the communities upon which they depend. The label "business," in fact, tends to obscure the dramatically different, much more personal, and inherently more tenuous circumstances that the owners of small businesses live with.

Our suggestion, therefore, is that future strategic planning dialogues focus on business as a fundamentally local enterprise, no matter how large the participating firms actually are. Even national and global corporations operate within local communities. Whereas consumers and policymakers experience large companies as powerful brands with paid lobbyists, community residents experience them as local employers and neighbors. We cannot equate them to small businesses directly because the financial contributions and brand stature of large corporations tend to dominate decision-making even within local trade associations and local Chambers of Commerce. That being said, however, the very public climate change and sustainability letter that BlackRock's chairman and CEO, Larry Fink, wrote to corporate CEOs in 2020 is applying pressure on public companies to shift their decision-making focus away from the desires of shareholders, exclusively, toward the interests of broader groups of stakeholders.[9] The ACE dialogue process can help accelerate this shift by bringing local small business leaders, local labor, and local corporate leaders together in multi-sectoral, community-level dialogues about equity and the climate crisis.

At their core, the processes that led to *An ACE Strategic Planning Framework for the United States* helped people from all walks of life set their professional and societal roles aside just enough to hear one another differently. They discovered both shared and divergent concerns, and collaborated on ways to make their communities more just, equitable, climate-smart, and resilient. In the next section, you will discover what this dialogue and review process is capable of achieving.

Chapter 4

An ACE National Strategic Planning Framework for the United States

Collaborative Contributions from the Nation's Diverse
ACE Community
Tom Bowman and Deb Morrison, writers
November 30, 2020

Executive Summary

Engaging, informing, and empowering the public to participate in solutions to the climate crisis is essential if humanity is to meet the urgency and scale of the challenge.

- A national strategic plan for public empowerment is needed to catalyze and accelerate a just transition to a low-carbon future. The Action for Climate Empowerment (ACE) agenda—as described by UNFCCC Article 6 and Article 12 of the Paris Agreement—enables all nations to inform, encourage, and empower their publics to design and implement their Nationally Determined Contributions (NDCs) to global climate action.
- With the adoption and implementation of an ACE national strategic plan, the United States would become the first major emitting country to fulfill a commitment to ACE. Such actions would help our nation rebuild its international reputation and become a global leader for rapid, equitable, just, and effective society-wide climate action.
- Moreover, such actions are crucial to ensuring that a post-COVID recovery accelerates climate action and rebuilds the economy in just, equitable, and sustainable ways.

An ACE National Strategic Planning Framework for the United States is intended to guide the completion of a national strategic plan in time for delivery at the 26th UNFCCC Conference of the Parties in November 2021.

- This Strategic Planning Framework was co-created by the U.S. ACE community through multi-decade efforts, which culminated in a series of participatory dialogues during August 2020 (see Appendix A and B). This document compiles the key principles, specific recommendations, and collective wisdom expressed by more than 150 participants who are affiliated with roughly 120 different organizations and networks. The participants represented a broad swath of the nation's ACE landscape and its tremendous diversity, experience, and geographic reach.
- While the ACE community's efforts have been invaluable to the nation, those efforts have been fragmented, and they have never been strategically aligned. An ACE national strategic plan that is co-created with diverse members of the ACE community will overcome a crucial barrier to meeting the climate crisis, namely, the low levels of public engagement and participation. A national strategy will, at last, align the ACE community's work and provide coherence and support to the nation's efforts to inform, encourage, and empower the public to make rapid progress on climate solutions.

THE U.S. ACE AGENDA:

- Acknowledges the deep history of learning and practice that has taken place in the ACE community.
- Weaves climate empowerment and public participation into every aspect of the nation's social, cultural, civic, and economic life.

- Is culturally relevant and highly salient to foster widespread commitments and support.
- Emphasizes local-level climate action and participation in decision-making.
- Recognizes and builds upon the diversity of knowledge, expertise, values, and ways of knowing and acting throughout society.
- Holds climate justice as inseparable from effective climate action. ACE calls for empowering Black, Indigenous, and People of Color (BIPOC); members of low-income communities; and all those on the social, environmental, and economic front lines of climate impacts to participate and lead.

Meeting the climate challenge will require transformative, structural changes in order to foster inclusive public participation and decision-making processes.

A U.S. ACE NATIONAL STRATEGY WOULD:

- Shift the focus of ACE activities from the actions of individuals to collective action.
- Shift decision-making processes from a model that seeks local input to a model that encompasses local participation, leadership, and consent.
- Create safe and meaningful pathways for BIPOC and low-income communities—which bear the greatest burdens of climate impacts—to participate and lead in decision-making.
- Reduce and remove barriers to effective action by community-scale actors and organizations. This includes reducing barriers to competition for adequate funding.
- Make financial investments through participatory processes that are guided by local concerns, research-

based evidence, and the priorities of BIPOC and low-income communities.

- Design policies in ways that enable and encourage cross-sector collaboration and coordination for climate action.
- Integrate ACE—especially education and training—into government purchasing and contracting policies.
- Integrate ACE into the climate action plans of all government agencies and line-item budgets.
- Develop climate messaging that is highly salient, simple, and pervasive.
- Increase financial support and sustained commitments to ACE.
- Develop and implement tools to monitor and evaluate progress on public empowerment and participation.

SUGGESTED URGENT ACTIONS:

- Insert the following language, or its equivalent, into the 2020 NDC to the UNFCCC:

The United States commits to nominate a National Focal Point for Action for Climate Empowerment (ACE) and establish a diverse ACE Task Team that will utilize the community-developed *An ACE National Strategic Planning Framework for the United States* to create an ACE national strategy for delivery at COP26 and follow through on its implementation.

- Establish a federal office for ACE, nominate a National Focal Point (NFP) for ACE, establish the ACE Task Team and its collaboration structures, and provide the authorities and support required to co-create the U.S. ACE national strategic plan with diverse members of the U.S. ACE community.

This Strategic Planning Framework is a non-partisan document. It is, however, the product of those who participated in its creation. Future strategic planning will need to bring additional voices into the dialogue process as well. Support must be provided, for example, to members of conservative and rural communities who might find the language of climate change problematic, yet for whom stewardship of the land and the wellbeing of their communities are deeply held values. Further dialogue opportunities should also be extended to members of the business, health, science, social science, and other stakeholder communities. These additional steps will help ensure that the ACE national strategy encompasses the diverse concerns of the nation.

An ACE national strategy will greatly accelerate a just transition to a low-carbon future. Members of the ACE community are ready to assist and support the development and implementation of an ACE national strategic plan for the United States.

I. Where Does the United States Stand on Climate Change?

The United States officially withdrew from the Paris Agreement on November 4, 2020. Over the preceding decades, however, numerous actions and programs within federal agencies have made substantial progress toward building understanding and capacity to respond to climate change within various sectors of society.[1] Likewise, states, cities, Tribal Nations, national and community-based non-profits, and private sector organizations have committed themselves to finding solutions. One assessment of climate commitments notes:

> American coalitions of states, cities, businesses, and others committed to climate action in support of the Paris Agreement are massive and globally significant. They now represent 68

percent of U.S. GDP, 65 percent of U.S. population and 51 percent of U.S. emissions. If they were a country, these U.S. coalitions would have the world's second largest economy — second only to the United States itself.[2]

These hope-inspiring commitments do not appear to be widely understood by the public.[3] Federal political leadership, in fact, has not delivered coherent messaging on climate change for many years. In a 2018 survey, only 6 percent of respondents said that humanity can and will reduce global warming, despite about half of the people in the United States saying that global warming could be reduced if appropriate actions are taken. The same survey found that only about one-third of the public — just 35 percent — talks about global warming with family and friends "often" or "occasionally."[4] Yet public concern about climate change reached an all-time high in 2020, with nearly 58 percent falling into the two most worried categories in the "Global Warming's Six Americas" survey.[5]

Such a wide gulf between high levels of concern and low levels of confidence is one of the reasons why the international community calls for a fundamental change in public engagement. Action for Climate Empowerment (ACE) goals, which are expressed in Article 6 of the United Nations Framework Convention on Climate Change (UNFCCC), focus on building public support and capacity for finding solutions and taking action on the climate crisis. UNESCO and UNFCCC Secretariat guidelines for implementing ACE explain that public empowerment is necessary in order to meet the challenges.

The solutions to the negative effects of climate change are also the paths to a safer, healthier, cleaner and more prosperous future for all. However, for such a future to become reality, citizens of all countries, at all levels of government, society and enterprise, need to understand and be involved.[6]

The ACE agenda (goals and recommended processes) involves marshalling creativity, initiative, and collaboration among communities, organizations, and individuals as the best way to accelerate a just transition to a low-carbon and resilient world. Article 12 of the Paris Agreement of 2015 calls on nations to actively pursue ACE:

> Parties shall cooperate in taking measures, as appropriate, to enhance climate change education, training, public awareness, public participation and public access to information, recognizing the importance of these steps with respect to enhancing action under this Agreement.[7]

At COP25 in 2019, several nations shared their work to accelerate ACE implementation. The need for such work was reaffirmed by the delegations.[8] In the United States, however, ACE is not yet central to policymakers' thinking about solving the climate crisis. Residents of low-income and rural communities and Black, Indigenous and People of Color (BIPOC), meanwhile, remain marginalized and largely excluded from policymaking about energy, pollution, education, and justice issues, even though they are being harmed disproportionately by the negative impacts of pollution and climate change.[9, 10] Policymaking processes rarely recognize the expertise that these populations contribute to climate action.

Public opinion about the priority of climate change in federal policymaking is split along party lines and has been diverging since the 1990s.[11] There is strong public support, however, for federal investments in renewable energy sources, generating renewable energy on public lands, providing tax rebates for energy-efficient vehicles and solar panels, regulating carbon dioxide as a pollutant, and the Green New Deal proposal.[12] Some of the components of public engagement, therefore, exist, yet public confidence and empowerment remain low. People have, in fact, been successfully dissuaded by intentional efforts to mislead and confuse them.[13]

Against this backdrop, the "ACE community" in the United States—meaning educators, communicators, researchers, social movements, community groups, and a wide range of others—are doing significant work.[14] They are skillful, hold deep knowledge, and feel a sense of great urgency about harnessing the strategic resources required to accelerate equitable and just climate action.

II. Why Create an ACE National Strategy?

As noted, UNFCCC Article 6 calls on signatory nations to empower their publics to become active participants in solving the climate challenge. This is the case because "The transition to a low emissions and resilient development requires individuals and communities to reach an unprecedented level of awareness, knowledge and skills."[15] As part of the 2012 UNFCCC Doha Work Programme, moreover, parties recommended that each nation develop a national strategy to achieve ACE goals. At COP24 in 2018, parties agreed:

'to continue to promote the systemic integration of gender-sensitive and participatory education, training, public awareness, public participation, public access to information, and regional and international cooperation into all mitigation and adaptation activities implemented under the Convention, as well as under the Paris Agreement, as appropriate, including into the processes of designing and implementing their nationally determined contributions' (Decision 17/CMA.1, paragraph 5).[16]

Thus, integrating a national strategic plan for ACE into periodic Nationally Determined Contributions (NDCs) is crucial. Creating and implementing an ACE national strategy will help the people of the United States participate in creating the policies and actions needed to meet the climate challenge. Doing so through inclusive processes that enhance climate justice and equity is necessary, as stated by the explicit alignment between the UNFCCC; U.N. Sustainable Development Goals; and the United Nations Education, Scientific and Cultural Organization's (UNESCO) deep history and trajectory of work in sustainability education.[17] Equity and empowerment are, in fact, inseparable from successful efforts to reduce carbon pollution and build resilience. The United Nations Declaration on the Rights of Indigenous Peoples (UNDRIP) provides further support for self-determination and informed consent, although the United States has not yet elevated this declaration of Indigenous rights to the status of binding law.[18]

As part of the commitment to ACE, each nation is expected to identify a National Focal Point (NFP) for developing and implementing an ACE national strategy (under the overall National Focal Point of the Party) and include ACE in NDCs. An NDC covering the 2020 to 2030 timeframe is due in 2020. As of the writing of this *Strategic Planning Framework*, the United States has not designated a National Focal Point, nor has an ACE national strategy been developed. On November 4, 2020, the U.S. officially withdrew from the Paris Agreement and has not submitted a 2020 NDC.

The United States has deep and diverse resources—communities, businesses, networks, organizations, institutions, and individuals—working to advance the ACE objectives, yet their efforts are not strategically coordinated or aligned.[19] Building an ACE national strategy will significantly enhance coordination and collaboration, create financial efficiencies, reduce duplication of effort, and improve the effectiveness of efforts to engage and empower the public in inclusive and equitable ways. Developing an ACE national strategy is a key step to accelerating climate actions in the United States.

III. Why Create an ACE National Strategic Planning Framework?

COP26, in November 2021, will be an important update on the Paris Agreement. Taking stock of global commitments will be based on revised NDCs from signatory nations, which are expected to include national strategies for ACE implementation. As noted, the U.S. is unlikely to submit a revised NDC in 2020, nor designate a National Focal Point for an ACE national strategy.

By its own initiative, the ACE community in the United States undertook this *Strategic Planning Framework* process in accordance with UNESCO and UNFCCC Secretariat ACE guidelines, in order to accelerate development of the first U.S. ACE national strategic plan in early 2021. The objective was to lay the groundwork by engaging the ACE community in an inclusive process and provide a roadmap for completing a national strategy in time for delivery at COP26.

Although this *Strategic Planning Framework* reflects the ACE community's contributions over many years, the *Strategic Planning Framework* project was initiated in late 2019 and the majority of the work was accomplished in the midst of the global COVID-19 pandemic. The strong commitments by all involved are founded on the shared understanding that a coordinated and strategic approach to the ACE agenda in the U.S. is critical to ensuring a post-COVID economic recovery that will accelerate climate action in just and equitable ways.

IV. What Does the ACE Framework Contribute?

The U.S. ACE community is now deeply engaged in a collaborative process to help develop a national strategy. The process of building the *Strategic Planning Framework* involved participants from 120 different organizations, institutions,[20] social movements, businesses, Tribes, and governments ranging from federal agencies to municipalities. This community is diverse, talented, experienced, and engaged in significant work.[21] Despite the community's participation in various professional networks and numerous gatherings over decades, however, their work, overall, has never been strategically aligned and coordinated in systematic ways.

To build the *Strategic Planning Framework*, participants engaged in four online dialogues based on the U.N.'s Talanoa Dialogue Platform[22] that were designed to bring people from different professions, geographies, and perspectives together. Through their collective contributions, the *Strategic Planning Framework* provides a coherent vision of where climate action and public empowerment efforts should be by 2030. The ACE community's inputs also reveal many different perspectives that are based on lived experience in a range of different contexts. For example, Indigenous participants stated that the right to self-determination requires the United States to honor past treaties and to seek actual consent—not just opinions—when considering energy and environmental policies. While deeply supporting the rights of BIPOC to equity, justice, and self-determination, the *Strategic Planning Framework* does not advocate for any participants' specific policy prescriptions. Instead, the *Strategic Planning Framework* articulates issues and viewpoints that must be addressed in the national strategy and in the strategic planning process.

Beyond stating a vision, the *Strategic Planning Framework* also offers specific recommendations in the six ACE elements: education, training, public awareness, public access to information, public participation, and international cooperation.[23] The recommendations are designed to overcome structural and often unintended obstacles, while making the most of opportunities to improve the efficacy and alignment of climate education, communication, and outreach[24] programs, policies, and initiatives. New approaches to improving collaboration, up-front and periodic evaluation, funding, and inclusive decision-making are clearly expressed in these recommendations.

The *Strategic Planning Framework* is not a strategic plan, however, so recognizing the limitations of its scope is important.

1. Guidelines from UNESCO and the UNFCCC Secretariat suggest that the National Focal Point inventory all federal and sub-national policies that can be improved through the incorporation of ACE goals and strategies. While the *Strategic Planning Framework* identifies connections to certain policies, the ACE community did not have the resources to conduct a comprehensive inventory.

2. ACE guidelines call for assessments of public knowledge, perceptions, and attitudes about climate change and climate solutions:

> Assess needs specific to national circumstances regarding implementation of Article 6 of the UNFCCC, using special research methods and other relevant instruments to determine target audiences and potential partnerships; and develop communication strategies on climate change based on targeted social research in order to create behavioural changes.[25]

The *Strategic Planning Framework* describes certain attributes of public knowledge and perceptions, but a full and complete assessment is beyond the scope of this project. Such an assessment would need to consider multiple methodologies in order to ensure that a comprehensive picture emerges and culturally responsive results are obtained.[26]

3. ACE guidelines call for inclusive consultations and decision-making processes involving all segments of society and its diverse ACE communities. The *Strategic Planning*

Framework accomplished a robust pilot project and, in so doing, identified gaps where additional dialogue will be needed.

For example, future engagement could expand dialogue with the business, labor, and health communities, which are crucial elements of the nation's climate response, but were not well represented in this process. Support should also be provided to members of conservative and rural communities who might find the language of climate change problematic, yet for whom stewardship of the land and the wellbeing of their communities are deeply held values.

While youth and BIPOC communities were engaged, there is considerable room for further dialogue and wider participation. Likewise, many individuals, organizations, and institutions that promote climate-friendly behaviors (for example, communication firms, public utilities, behavioral scientists, natural scientists, environmental and educational NGOs) will have more to contribute to the national strategy. These additional steps will help ensure that the ACE national strategy fully addresses the diverse concerns of the nation.

Given these caveats, the *Strategic Planning Framework* and its processes provide (1) a shared vision from the ACE community, (2) key recommendations for policy implementation, (3) identification of key concerns among various ACE communities that the national strategy must address, (4) a practical model for community engagement using the U.N.'s Talanoa Dialogue Platform combined with strategic review, and (5) guidance on specific needs for further dialogue and engagement in order to complete a U.S. ACE national strategic plan.

V. The U.S. National Circumstances

UNESCO and UNFCCC Secretariat guidelines urge nations to develop national strategies for public empowerment according to their national circumstances. The circumstances for ACE action in the United States are inherently complex, distributed, and diverse. The United States is a country in which decentralized authority is both structural and cultural. It is a nation that shares decision-making among multiple branches of Tribal, federal, state, and local governments, and some segments of society are excluded from decision-making processes altogether. It has a multi-cultural society that often celebrates individual liberty, individual initiative, free enterprise, and individual responsibility. Because such ideals are not universally held by all cultural groups,[27] compliance with and fidelity to coordinated strategies will rely heavily on individual stakeholder commitments to, and participation in, the design of strategies, policies, reporting protocols, and other measures.[28]

In school-based education, for example, national principles for climate and energy literacy were developed by a network of educators, scientists, and stakeholders in 13 federal agencies.[29] New approaches such as "justice-centered phenomena" have been shown to make climate science more relevant to students and improve educational outcomes.[30] These principles, in combination with *A Framework for K-12 Science Education*[31] and the *Next Generation Science Standards*,[32] are highly influential, yet individual states can choose to adopt all or part of national guidelines or develop guidelines of their own. Curriculum and textbooks are written with multiple standards in mind.

Additionally, education funding also varies according to the financial circumstances of the various states. As a result, access to climate education is at least partly conditioned by the financial capacities of the states. While federal funding for education is guided, at least in part, by achievement according to standards-based tests, the states and districts retain authority over curriculum, textbooks, and the creation and administration of testing in their jurisdictions. Because funding and decision-making in education are distributed across multiple jurisdictions, there is a lack of coherence in climate education.

The leading programs in climate-related workforce development and training, community-based education, and the other ACE elements are equally decentralized. A large number of informal networks, professional societies, trade associations, and other types of organizations develop and manage climate- and energy-related learning programs of their own design according to their own standards and theories of societal change.

Justice-centered environmental and climate networks have been working on ACE activities for a long time.[33] Meanwhile, a growing number of other community-based organizations that focus on ACE activities have deepened their commitments to social and environmental justice.[34] Such ACE activities have been and continue to be undertaken by those in both paid and volunteer roles. Framing ACE work as justice work is also an emerging and important direction in academic research.[35] The ACE community agrees that justice principles need to be integral to ACE work.

Six attributes specific to the U.S. require further attention.

1. *Awakening to Climate Justice*—The United States is a nation in which BIPOC have been and continue to be disenfranchised and discriminated against, and in many cases, removed from their lands. The history of forced movements of BIPOC communities has harmed generations of people over time. Moreover, low-income and BIPOC neighborhoods, communities, institutions, and individuals are exposed to more environmental health risks, such as pollution, heat stress, flooding, and extreme weather, than are affluent populations.[36] Economic, educational, social, and political opportunities are far less available to BIPOC populations than to white and generally more affluent populations.[37] The ACE community understands that the wide disparities

in health outcomes and opportunities—and ever-widening income inequality[38]—are unjust and unsustainable. A national ACE strategy and the processes through which it is developed and implemented must embrace a paradigm shift—a fundamental break from the colonialism, anti-Blackness, Indigenous invisibility, racism, patriarchy, and English language dominance[39] that have oppressed BIPOC people, communities, and governments in the United States and abroad.

Accordingly, the ACE community recognizes that transformative structural changes are necessary, and that ACE-related policies that fail to address inequity and injustice will, themselves, fail. The ACE process is not merely about adjusting existing power relationships. ACE is grounded in the recognition that different power relationships, knowledge, and practices already exist throughout society. ACE strategies and planning processes, therefore, must recognize that diversity and differences are assets, and that just and equitable partnerships and policies will enable everyone to engage and share power equitably, and benefit from the resulting opportunities.

The ACE strategic planning process must also recognize that diverse groups of people, as well as individuals within those groups, have different views and perspectives about climate goals and solutions. For example, some BIPOC leaders call for the U.S. to become a zero-emissions society, not a net-zero society, because the latter goal allows for the continued use of fossil fuels and, therefore, a continuation of disproportionately poor health for BIPOC communities. The zero-emissions goal reflects the widespread view within the ACE community that decolonizing[40] decision-making processes requires that the U.S. honor existing treaties with Indigenous nations and seek consent, not merely advice, when making energy and climate-related policies. Many people, including people in the BIPOC community, have called for accountability on the part of polluters, and an end to the extraordinary influence polluters have in governance that allows pollution to continue as a default in people's expectations.

2. *Increasing Public Concern about Climate Change*—People's concern about the climate crisis has been increasing over the past five years, at least. The number of people who say they are alarmed has grown by 15 percentage points since 2015, while the number of people who are dismissive of the issue has decreased by five points.[41] There is strong evidence that a confluence of factors is driving engagement, including, among other things, an increase in people's lived experience with extreme weather events and the amplification of the voices of trusted messengers other than climate scientists and environmentalists. These trusted voices include doctors who have been speaking out about climate-related health harms that people and communities are actually experiencing,[42, 43] and weathercasters who have been validating the reality of the climate crisis.[44] As a result, climate change is being repositioned in the minds of the public from an abstract and distant risk to an immediately relevant and concrete threat. An ACE national strategy will be strengthened by a reliance on social science research to identify factors that are likely to motivate public engagement and validate the efficacy of communication campaigns.

3. *Youth-Centered Education and Social Movements*—Young people learn about climate change, climate justice, and social justice more broadly in school and in a variety of other contexts, but there is a lack of coherence across jurisdictions. The quality and extent of climate education is uneven in the U.S., and it is tied closely to the knowledge and political

views of the educators that youth encounter.[45]

Meanwhile, the growing youth climate movement, which is largely coordinated and expanded through social media, calls for accelerated action and reform of climate-related learning opportunities.[46] The redesign of educational resources, however, will require more than a focus on climate science. Since educational institutions and curricula have long perpetuated colonial thinking and power structures,[47] a paradigm shift is necessary. Young people need, and in some cases are calling for, active, solutions-oriented science, social studies, and media literacy education that emphasizes systems-thinking approaches to learning about environmental and social interconnections as part of broader civics education.

4. *COVID-19 Impacts*—The COVID-19 crisis is a defining feature of policymaking today and is likely to remain so in the coming years. Recovery from the pandemic represents a unique opportunity to organize and direct investments in climate solutions, justice, communities, and public empowerment.[48] For example, investments in green infrastructure, workforce development, and alignment of subject matter in climate and climate justice education can work together more effectively than they have in the past.[49]

5. *Overcommunication and Competition for Attention*—By any measure, people are bombarded by more messages today than at any other time in human history. According to a 2013 report in *Science Daily*, 90 percent of the world's data had been generated in the previous two years.[50] Various reports place the number of messages the average person receives between 5,000 and 10,000 per day.[51] The implications for ACE strategies in the U.S. are profound because effective messages will need to be salient enough, engaging enough,

simple enough, and sufficiently aligned with the things people care about to gain attention in a highly competitive communication environment.[52]

6. *Intentional Disinformation and Dissuasion*—Governments and the people of the United States have been subjected to well-documented, decades-long campaigns to mislead and misinform them, and dissuade them from seeking and implementing solutions to the climate crisis. Funded largely by fossil fuel interests and ideological libertarian individuals and organizations, these campaigns have generated misleading pseudo-scientific reports, attacked individual scientists and the scientific enterprise as a whole, asserted narratives that global warming is not dangerous while climate solutions will cause economic suffering, prioritized individual actions and liberty over collective action, written draft legislation favorable to the fossil fuel industry, challenged climate-related policies in court, and more.[53, 54] These efforts have been effective: according to a 2018 study, 46 percent of the U.S. population thinks that global warming can be reduced, but only 6 percent believes that humanity will do what is necessary.[55] These views are reflected around the world, especially in industrialized nations. The 2019 version of the international Edelman Trust Barometer survey found widespread pessimism that humanity will be better off in five years' time, while the overwhelming majority said that "the system" is not working for them.[56] As a result, addressing intentional disinformation and its harmful effects must be incorporated into national strategic planning for ACE.

As mentioned, ACE work in the United States has expanded significantly in recent years through youth movements, initiatives in formal and informal education, workforce training, and civic engagement.[57] Taken together, these attributes explain why the ACE community believes that an ACE national strategy must encourage collective action and not rely entirely on the actions of individuals. The ACE community also understands that a national strategy will be inherently iterative and dynamic because the circumstances in which ACE policies are implemented are dynamic.

In such a context, the UNESCO and UNFCCC Secretariat guidelines' call for inclusive decision-making processes is crucial to success. The U.S. ACE national strategy must articulate a compelling and coherent vision that empowers all stakeholders. ACE policies, moreover, must embrace the nation's rich diversity without imposing the dominant values systems and worldviews that offend or disenfranchise various constituencies. The goal is to weave climate action, justice, meaningful involvement, fair treatment, and empowerment into the social and decision-making fabric across an extraordinarily diverse society.

VI. The U.S. ACE Community's Vision

Diverse members of the ACE community in the United States used a back-casting process[58] to establish a vision for where the nation should be in 2030. This is the initial timeframe for ACE national strategies. In the ACE community's view, the adoption of the recommendations put forth in this document will help the United States achieve a number of crucial goals for climate action, and for the conduct of ACE work as well.

1. *The U.S. is a leader in identifying and implementing climate solutions.* These solutions are powered by universal and inclusive community and civic engagement. Civic engagement is expressed by a number of different accomplishments, including the following:

   a. Actions by government agencies, communities, private sector organizations, and individuals demonstrate a society-wide commitment to climate solutions.

b. The social ethos for action is justice- and solutions-oriented and conveys a broadly held sense of urgency.

c. Every government has implemented a climate action and disaster preparedness plan that includes budget line items for climate action, coordination, education, and other priorities.

d. Decision-making and policymaking are accomplished through the participation of all concerned community members. Decision-making processes combine top-down coordination with bottom-up representation and action. The widespread participation reflects a high level of trust and mutual respect which, in turn, enables productive partnerships among members of the public, community organizations, elected officials, and businesses.

e. Elected representatives are more accountable to the public on climate, energy, and public health issues. Public access to information and universal access to electronic communication provide the public with very high levels of accountability.

f. With strong public support, the U.S. has placed a ban on new fossil fuel development.

g. People feel national pride about U.S. leadership on climate action.

h. The U.S. has earned a positive international reputation for its collaborative public participation and decision-making.

2. *Equity and justice are inseparable from climate action.* The United States has built transparent processes for inclusive decision-making that recognizes expertise in BIPOC, low-income, and rural communities; substantially elevates their leadership; and provides resources for meaningful participation. These processes allow those who have traditionally been

disenfranchised to feel safe and valued as they engage in meaningful decision-making and collaboration.

a. Climate and social justice training is standard practice for all policymakers.

b. Federal and state governments have aligned policymaking with ACE goals, which include BIPOC, youth, and gender representation at all levels of decision-making.

c. Multiple perspectives on decision-making processes have replaced traditional colonial, patriarchal, white perspectives as the unspoken default assumptions.

d. BIPOC, youth, and diverse genders are fully integrated into governance structures in government, business, philanthropy, and other aspects of public and civic life.

e. Members of other low-income and rural communities who have historically had relatively little political and economic power have been invited and received the financial support necessary to be integrated into dialogue and decision-making processes.

f. The U.S. has established international, national, Indigenous, and sub-national processes for sharing and expanding the adoption of effective practices in culturally sensitive and appropriate ways.

3. *Rapid decarbonization of the U.S. economy is driven by a climate-ready workforce.* People in all jobs are aware of and attentive to sustainable solutions.

a. Workers at every level of the economy approach their jobs through a climate solutions lens that integrates sustainability goals into the everyday fabric of the workplace.

b. Climate solutions, communication, and resilience

are included in career and technical education and in professional development opportunities throughout the economy.

c. Climate solutions provide a rubric for aligning workforce education with in-service technical training.

d. Training and career development opportunities ensure equitable access to jobs for all people.

4. *New levels of transparency, accountability, and collaboration have established strong public trust in climate-related decision-making.*

a. Those who are negatively impacted by environmental harms — pollution, extreme weather, and climate change — are prioritized in decision-making. This means that municipal, state, and federal policymaking actively facilitates participation by those who are affected the most. Under-resourced communities are supported by trustworthy mechanisms that ensure their participation and prioritize their interests.

b. The requirement for public consent has replaced the financial and power dynamics that favor the interests of polluters over those of local populations.

c. The combination of climate solutions, climate justice, and community consent and control are a dominant lens through which leaders approach policymaking.

5. *Lifelong learning that is both wide and deep[59] is integrated into local communities and helps accelerate a just transition to a sustainable future.*

a. Educators and communicators are engaged in continual professional learning in order to better serve the public.

b. Education about climate solutions, resilience, and civic

engagement is inseparable from climate action plans. Such education must address the historic and geopolitical dimensions of the climate crisis.

c. A wider definition of a "well-educated person" involves awareness of and meaningful relationships with different approaches to knowledge, including local and Indigenous knowledge, practices, and ways of knowing. This wider definition recognizes the different values in rural, BIPOC, urban, and other communities.

6. *Progress on these accomplishments is measured by multiple types of quantitative and qualitative metrics.*

a. Assessments capture the contributions of individuals, organizations, and communities rather than national statistics alone.

b. Metrics are culturally responsive to diverse communities and contexts. This includes Indigenous methods and cross-sectoral input.[60]

The ACE Community's vision for 2030 also describes where the conduct of ACE-related work should be in 2030. Whereas the community's work is currently fragmented, by 2030 their efforts would allow strong strategic alignment in support of the vision for the nation as described above. Additionally, the work of an expanded and growing ACE community is characterized by the following attributes.

1. *ACE decisions are evidence-based according to metrics that reflect proven effectiveness.*

2. *ACE messages and public education are both widespread and pervasive in the news, media, the arts, schools, community-based learning, and elsewhere.*

3. *Decision-making about ACE projects and funding is inclusive and equitable.* A wide variety of institutions, including those in formal and informal education, business, and government, are proactive about removing institutional racism, sexism, classism, and other forms of oppression.

4. *The United States has mapped ACE resources and established strong support for productive collaboration among government, science, education, communication, and business.*

    a. The collaboration infrastructure supports shared goals for communication, education, and public engagement in ways that meet the needs of local communities.
    b. Diverse models for community-based action and BIPOC leadership drive locally grounded learning.
    c. Collaboration among formal and informal education institutions, media organizations, businesses, non-governmental organizations, and government agencies support community-level, project-based learning about climate solutions and resilience.
    d. Collaborative ACE work is focused on the needs and interests of local communities.

5. *Learning systems and literacy standards reflect the values expressed in this vision statement.*

    a. Literacy in formal and informal education focuses on equity, justice, and empowerment in the exercise of personal, community-level, and political rights and responsibilities.
    b. Education prioritizes local connections to ecosystem-wide and global phenomena, such as climate change, and solutions to global crises.
    c. Education prioritizes systems-thinking approaches

to addressing climate change and the interconnections between disciplines.

d. Multi-disciplinary learning about climate change has been embraced at all levels of formal education.

e. Cultural literacy, gender responsiveness, youth empowerment, science-based decision-making, and social-emotional learning[61] are integrated into formal and informal education.

f. Educational institutions are included in community resilience activities.

g. Cultural institutions such as museums, aquariums, zoos, nature centers, and community centers enjoy high levels of public trust for accelerating the development of community-based climate solutions.

h. An examination of the values systems underlying education systems leads to transformative changes.

VII. Strategic Recommendations

One of the most effective ways to engage people with climate solutions and empower them to act is by incorporating the ACE elements into activities that are already taking place. The UNESCO/UNFCCC Secretariat guidelines, in fact, urge nations to build national strategies, in part, by integrating the six ACE elements—education, training, public awareness, public access to information, public participation, and regional and international cooperation—into existing laws, regulations, investments and grants, and decision-making processes. Building public education and empowerment into ongoing activities is potentially more efficient than developing an ACE national strategy as an entirely separate, stand-alone enterprise.

The ACE guidelines equally urge nations to inventory existing programs, organizations, and initiatives that address climate empowerment, assess their effectiveness, and find ways to support and amplify those that are working especially well.

While a national ACE strategy will require the United States—its governments, philanthropic foundations, and businesses—to make new investments and build some entirely new, targeted capabilities, the ACE agenda seeks to weave climate empowerment into the deeper social fabric.

According to the ACE community, both the integration of ACE into existing governance and the creation of new capabilities should be guided by four key principles that bring ACE guidance into the U.S. context. These principles apply to all six ACE elements. A discussion of additional recommendations concerning each specific ACE element will follow with the assumption that these, too, should reflect the key principles.

Key Principles

1. *Inclusive and Locally Focused Decision-making*—Public engagement and empowerment need to be rooted in listening to people's priorities rather than telling people what to do. As decision scientist Baruch Fischhoff wrote in 2007, those who design climate education, communication, and outreach programs must guard against overestimating their own effectiveness:

> People overestimate how widely their values are shared... People overestimate how widely their knowledge is shared...People overestimate how clearly they communicate...Research protects scientists and citizens against such imperfect intuitions...Communicating entails listening as well as speaking. Research provides a way to do that listening.[62]

Communication strategist Robert Gould observes that while most social campaigns try to convince their target audiences what they should do and how they should feel, the most successful social marketing campaigns are those that do not try to educate or convince the audience, but genuinely connect with them. He notes that top-down messaging is less effective than listening to people and providing knowledge and tools for them to share with their peers:

> The fuel of social change is horizontal, not vertical, influence. As the rise of social media makes clear, people don't respond to the powers that be, they respond to each other. Arm them with relevant content to share and signals to display. It's the secret of generating awareness, setting new agendas for policymakers and creating new social norms.[63]

These observations by social scientists make it clear that the ACE agenda involves dynamic relationships among people who have different points of view and who live and work in different circumstances. The ACE guidelines specifically emphasize inclusive and community-driven decision-making processes, and recognize that, "In some places, this will prompt profound changes in how political leaders and civil servants are accustomed to working and encourage people to be more attentive to policy-making."[64, 65]

As noted, the U.N. Talanoa Dialogue Platform provides a crucial methodology for diverse stakeholders to listen to one another, learn, and build trust. This *Framework* was built using such a dialogue process. Participants came together from many different perspectives and professions and set aside familiar transactional conversations in order to hear one another's values and concerns, and discover the elements of shared purpose. In his book, *The Magic of Dialogue*, social scientist Daniel Yankelovich describes how important this type of process is:

In traditional hierarchical arrangements, those at the top of the pecking order can afford to be casual about how well they understand those at lower levels. When people are more equal, they are obligated to make a greater effort to understand each other. If no one is the undisputed boss anymore, and if all insist on having their views respected, it follows that people must understand each other. You don't really have a voice if those making the decisions aren't prepared to listen to you.[66]

This approach to working in and with stakeholder communities is also consistent with and supported by justice-framed academic research in the learning sciences[67] and organizational change.[68]

RECOMMENDATIONS ABOUT INCLUSIVE AND LOCALLY FOCUSED DECISION-MAKING:

a. The ACE national strategy should establish a long-term dialogue capacity for climate-related decision-making at the community and regional levels. The ACE community recognizes that municipal governance is largely built around creating action plans, so space must be intentionally created in order to transcend transactional negotiations and allow sufficient time for people to develop mutual understanding and trust.

b. Designate a National Focal Point (NFP) for ACE, as required under the UNFCCC process, and require the NFP to establish and support ongoing cross-cutting and multi-sector dialogue processes with the ACE community itself (including educators, researchers, philanthropic organizations, communication practitioners, community groups, leaders of social movements, business, etc.).

c. The two previous recommendations reflect an urgent

need to bring local knowledge and experience into decision-making. The ACE agenda recognizes that people experience the impacts of climate change, and also take action, where they live. Strategic decision-making, therefore, should combine effective coordination and relationship building.

d. Effective local programs should be identified, and their visions and methodologies should be championed, shared, and taken up in new locations. While the mitigation contributions of individual community-based programs might appear to be relatively small, they also transform people's and communities' relationships to the climate crisis. The NFP should develop assessment tools that capture and aggregate the collective achievements of local actions throughout the nation.

2. *Equity and Justice in ACE Decision-making and Climate Solutions* — Climate justice and climate solutions are one and the same thing. The ACE community recognizes that colonial thinking is a driving force in the climate crisis, and that unjust processes will necessarily lead to unjust outcomes.[69]

Equity and inclusion can no longer be side conversations about climate solutions. The term "inclusion," in fact, strikes many people as a euphemism for "assimilation." This is neither the U.S. ACE community's intention, nor that of the UNFCCC. Instead, inclusion means shared power and structures that ensure equitable and meaningful involvement in all aspects of ACE work. The national strategy, therefore, should place equity and inclusion at the center of climate solutions and ensure a safe environment for BIPOC participation in discussions and decision-making.

RECOMMENDATIONS FOR EQUITY AND JUSTICE IN ACE
DECISION-MAKING AND CLIMATE SOLUTIONS:

a. The ACE national strategy should establish diversity
requirements for decision-making boards and committees
in civic governance, philanthropy, and corporate affairs,
and in developing and implementing the ACE national
strategic plan.

b. The public comment model should be shifted away
from one that gathers opinions to one that requires the
consent of BIPOC communities and Tribal Nations. The
ACE community understands that this recommendation
includes a call for the United States to honor treaties with
Tribal Nations. Members of the ACE community agree
that decisions about policies that would encourage fossil
fuel extraction on public lands or investments in carbon
capture and storage in order to prolong the use of fossil
fuels, for example, should not be made without the consent
of the low-income and BIPOC communities where people
are already suffering the most severe health and ecological
consequences of fossil fuel pollution and climate change.

c. The United States should ratify the United Nations
Declaration on the Rights of Indigenous Peoples (UNDRIP).

d. Evaluation of policy performance should include non-
colonial methodologies, such as the Most Significant
Change[70] approach supported by USAID and the Mauri
Model,[71] in order to help ensure equity and inclusiveness
in measurement outcomes.

e. In addition to assessing changes in public understanding
and perceptions, the ACE NFP should incorporate metrics
about natural ecosystems and human health: clean air,
clean water, changes to the built environment, and changes
to manufacturing practices.[72]

f. The NFP and the ACE national strategy should encourage

scientists, educators, businesses, governments, and others to proactively engage with BIPOC communities and provide resources to support locally prioritized grassroots efforts.

3. *Evidence-based, Collaborative Planning and Decision-making*— Too many ACE-related programs are designed within single professions or according to the perspectives of the designers and their organizations. A strategic approach to public empowerment requires a shift to evidence-based planning and decision-making. Fischhoff describes a crucial feature of evidence-based planning:

> It is impossible to judge people fairly or to provide them with needed information without knowing what is on their minds when they formulate, resolve, implement, and revise climate-related choices.[73]

Understanding audiences is crucial, yet institutional guidelines and capabilities often take precedence in outreach planning and funding. These errors can be overcome through in-depth interactions among people at the local level, combined with collaborative research to yield a more complete picture:

> Climate science is needed to focus on choices that matter and get the facts right. Decision science is needed to identify the facts that should matter most when people evaluate their options. Social science is needed to describe people's perceptions of those critical facts, as well as their goals when making choices.[74]

As Fischhoff notes, research to understand target audiences is crucial and requires more than one professional perspective.

This means that decisions about design and investment in public outreach should be guided by processes that will create a deeper understanding of target audiences than is typically the case today.

Additionally, *Strategic Planning Framework* dialogue participants emphasize that the perspectives of professional researchers are not always sufficient. The ACE community points out the critical importance of local knowledge and different cultural and Indigenous ways of knowing. Local communities possess information that is needed in order to develop just and efficient resilience projects.[75] They also hold the relationships, rights, and interests that will determine whether mitigation strategies are both just and effective. Designing policies that people will embrace and implement requires genuinely inclusive collaboration and the consent of those who will be impacted by the decisions.

Clearly, evidence-based decision-making requires careful gathering of appropriate and actionable evidence. Some of the most effective intervention programs underway today were designed around assessments of who people trust for information about climate change, from whom they receive such information, how they interact with new information, what they already know and believe, and how they are influenced by other people whom they know.[76]

RECOMMENDATIONS FOR EVIDENCE-BASED,[77] COLLABORATIVE DECISION-MAKING:

a. The ACE national strategy should encourage the development and implementation of robust audience evaluation practices for government agencies, philanthropic institutions, and the range of ACE actors as a fundamental criterion for decision-making.
b. The national strategy should encourage the development

and implementation of robust evaluation standards for ACE initiatives in order to measure their effectiveness so that adjustments can be made where necessary.

c. The national strategy should encourage the development and implementation of needs-based research so that results can be applied to ACE activities by funders and ACE actors more effectively and with greater confidence.

d. The NFP should make periodic assessments of the ACE national strategy and its implementation in order to report progress to the UNFCCC and the U.S. ACE community. Procedures should be established to update the national strategy as needed.

4. *Access to Sustained Financial Support*—Achieving ACE goals will require higher levels of sustained funding from a variety of sources for public education, communication, outreach, and empowerment. Funding decisions should be made according to a coordinated national strategy. This means that decisions should be evidence-based, as described above, that decision-making processes should be inclusive and just, and that decisions should be made according to the strategic merit of proposed initiatives.

A second guideline is that decision-making about ACE investments should shift away from top-down approaches, which tend to focus on the largest potential reductions in greenhouse gas emissions as the only metric. Decision-making should lean toward people-related and community-scale projects that, in aggregate, will contribute significant emissions reductions while also engaging larger numbers of people in productive action. Redistributing ACE investments in this way should focus on equity, recognizing that the United States will be a BIPOC-majority society in the coming decades. The recommendations below identify some specific ways to make funding decisions more inclusive and equitable.

A third guideline is to lean funding away from the production of products and toward the processes of connecting with audiences. Community-level engagement is inherently process-oriented. The ACE community recommends that process-based metrics be employed to validate expenditures that are meant to increase the capacity of people and communities to create and implement solutions to the climate crisis.

RECOMMENDATIONS FOR ACCESS TO SUSTAINED FINANCIAL SUPPORT:

a. The national strategy should encourage the alignment of funding for ACE programs to be responsive to each program's implementation timeline rather than the funder's financial cycles. This will allow initiatives to more fully meet the objectives they are designed to achieve.

b. The national strategy should encourage the creation of funding pathways for BIPOC and low-income communities to pursue locally guided climate actions. The ACE community also recognizes that BIPOC and low-income communities may also work at regional, state, and national levels.

c. The national strategy should call upon funders to simplify grant application and administration processes. The ACE community reports that many community-based and BIPOC organizations are unfamiliar with the grant application process, often struggle to stay informed about funding opportunities, or lack the resources to compete equitably.

d. The national strategy should encourage or require greater BIPOC representation on the boards and decision-making committees of funding organizations.

e. The national strategy should increase funding to

sustain the infrastructure of ACE organizations, such as community groups. At present, funding tends to focus on new, innovative pilot projects, but does not support the infrastructure—salaries, rent, benefits, administrative costs, and so on—that would allow experienced ACE actors to remain engaged in ACE-related work.

f. The national strategy should increase and sustain funding for backbone coordination by multi-sector and multi-organization networks that support knowledge sharing and collaboration. At present, funding tends to support individual actors and organizations, but not the collaborative networks that are urgently needed.

g. As noted in the previous section, the national strategy should support increased funding for target audience evaluation and in-depth interactions with local ACE actors in order to increase the efficacy of ACE activities.

h. The national strategy should prioritize taking effective pilot projects to scale. At present, much more funding is available to test new concepts than to build successful concepts into full-scale programs. The nation will benefit from deploying proven ACE initiatives at significantly larger scales.

i. The United States should use the recovery from the COVID-19 pandemic to increase funding for ACE and integrate these principles and recommendations into government and philanthropic funding processes.

Recommendations Specific to Each ACE Element

1. *Education Recommendations—"Education enables people to understand the causes and consequences of climate change, to make informed decisions and to take appropriate actions to address it."*[78]

THE ACE NATIONAL STRATEGY SHOULD:

a. Integrate the relevance of climate change and climate solutions into all fields of study in school- and university-based education, not only science, technology, education, and math (STEM) fields. The ACE community recognizes that there is a difference between education about climate change and education for climate action. Knowledge that is disassociated with building the capacity to make informed decisions and take action is incomplete and insufficient. Integrating climate relevance into all fields, including civics, is intended to support education for climate action.
b. Increase funding and organizational support for interdisciplinary climate education.
c. Build data literacy into K-12 education as a fundamental skill for informed decision-making.
d. Incentivize school districts to appoint climate justice coordinators at the district level to help increase the capacity of educators and ensure that climate and climate justice curricula are implemented.[79] Coordinators should foster partnerships between K-12, higher, and informal education, and other organizations.
e. Develop and deploy curricula that approach climate change and climate solutions from a climate justice perspective.
f. Develop and deploy curricula that connect the local, regional, and global implications of climate change. There is strong evidence that local behaviors and impacts have the greatest salience to people.[80] The ACE community calls for an increased focus on place-based and intergenerational approaches to climate education.
g. Develop and deploy curricula about climate solutions. As one participant noted, "I've earned three advanced degrees and I don't know what to do."

h. Develop and deploy curricula to enhance systems thinking about climate change and other environmental issues.[81]

i. Train educators to use socio-emotional learning practices to help students cope with the traumatic nature of climate change.

j. Support the integration of Indigenous values, knowledge, and ways of knowing into climate change and environmental curricula. Develop curricula in collaboration with Tribal Nations.

k. Encourage investment in broadband access in low-income and rural communities and Tribal Nations, where online access is limited.

l. Support extending climate change education beyond the classroom through interactions with local ecosystems and by providing opportunities for students to become involved in climate solutions.

m. Empower educators—both teachers and educators in informal learning institutions (museums, aquariums, zoos, nature centers, and cultural centers)—to be key voices for advancing climate knowledge beyond the classroom. One goal of the ACE national strategy is to overcome the separation people experience between science and their lives outside the classroom.[82]

n. Prioritize equitable access to educational opportunities. For example, the COVID-19 pandemic has revealed deep inequities in access to online learning.

o. Elevate BIPOC as leaders in formal and informal education settings. The national strategy should address the low representation of BIPOC in STEM fields.

p. Increase BIPOC representation in educational decision-making processes.

q. Prioritize investments in educational infrastructure in low-income communities in order to help people meet basic needs, such as food, childcare, and transportation, that otherwise inhibit learning.

r. Incentivize community-based learning institutions to become focal points for community engagement, learning, and dialogue.

s. Incentivize informal learning institutions to focus on education about solutions to the climate crisis and help people put learning into practice.

t. Deploy COVID-19 relief and recovery funds to ensure that informal learning institutions survive the economic crisis and remain viable in their communities.

THE ACE NATIONAL FOCAL POINT SHOULD:

a. Survey teachers' understandings, perceptions, and ideological perspectives regarding climate change, climate justice, climate action, and the teaching of these. The survey should also identify obstacles that teachers face when teaching about climate change.

b. Refine existing and develop new pre- and in-service programs to improve educator confidence and ensure widespread climate learning throughout formal education systems.

c. Survey informal learning institutions about their capacity and level of comfort in giving people information about climate solutions. The national strategy should help informal institutions find ways to address visitor interest in climate solutions.

d. Help the education community identify and address forms of oppression by using interdisciplinary learning models in teaching about colonialism and Euro-centric worldviews.

2. *Training Recommendations — "Training provides the core*

technical and soft skills as well as advanced knowledge needed to support the transition to green economies and sustainable, inclusive climate-neutral and resilient societies."[83]

THE ACE NATIONAL STRATEGY SHOULD:

a. Focus on building the knowledge and skills needed to reduce greenhouse gas emissions and increase resilience in the next decade.

b. Standardize accreditation criteria and climate skills outcomes for all workforce development programs.

c. Require workforce training in climate-relevant skills, plus support for internships and technical education curricula in government contracts for infrastructure development projects.

d. Prioritize investment in emergency preparedness and response training nationwide.

e. Support and amplify existing in-service training agendas, such as the C40 Mayors Agenda,[84] the American Society of Civil Engineers training agenda,[85] and similar efforts.

f. Align K-12 and technical and career education with skills for climate-related jobs and participation in civic decision-making.

g. Prioritize training in cross-cultural and engagement skills.

h. Prioritize gender, income, BIPOC, and other forms of equity in the development of workforce training initiatives, including the selection of trainers and recipients of training.

i. Invest in and provide training for local community centers, which tend to bring people together and marshal their energy and commitments.

j. Similarly, build long-term funding models for community

organizations and environmental justice groups to provide workforce development and wrap-around services, such as soft skills job training, social services, job placement, and counseling.

k. Ensure equitable access to climate-related internships by requiring that they pay a reasonable wage to cover the costs of housing, transportation, and childcare. Without such provisions, climate training will only be available to a wealthier, predominantly white workforce.

l. Provide financial support to non-profit organizations in order to compensate interns appropriately.

m. Develop and deploy workforce training to help people address the socio-emotional aspects of climate change.

n. Incentivize the training of executives and educators to see all jobs through a climate lens. Such training should focus on resource efficiency (energy, water, food, materials), resilience strategies, and soft skills such as management processes and social services. As one participant put it, "The bad news is that we have a lot of work to do. The good news is that there is plenty of work for everyone to do."

o. Develop and deploy training for policymakers, business executives, and philanthropic institutions for inclusive decision-making processes that are adapted to the characteristics of the communities they serve.

p. Encourage a reexamination of professional cultures and their reward systems in order to reduce the disconnect between the dispassionate presentation of technical information versus caring about the future.[86]

THE ACE NATIONAL FOCAL POINT SHOULD:

a. Coordinate climate-relevant career pathways beginning at the grade levels where career identification begins.

b. Coordinate climate-relevant career pathways for mid-career professionals.

c. Develop metrics to track trends in the growth of green jobs and climate training across the economy.

d. Develop metrics to track the integration of climate action into non-green sector jobs.

e. Coordinate with labor unions to integrate climate-relevant skills into workforce development.

3. *Public Awareness Recommendations*—*"Successful public awareness campaigns engage communities and individuals in the common effort needed to foster climate-friendly behavior, sustainable lifestyles and implement national, regional, sectoral and international climate change policies."*[87]

THE ACE NATIONAL STRATEGY SHOULD:

a. Increase funding for public communication about climate change, public health, and climate solutions.

b. Include development of nationwide and regional strategic messaging campaigns to overcome persistent barriers such as a lack of efficacy and clarity, address critical gaps in knowledge, generate realistic hope about the paths forward, and help people see their own roles in these paths.[88]

c. Emphasize the need for additional trusted messengers—doctors, weathercasters, clergy, and others—to build confidence and counter disinformation campaigns.

d. Include a robust strategic and coordinated capacity to counter ongoing and possibly intensified efforts to misinform the public about the risks and costs of climate solutions.

e. Recognize that confidence in solutions is built through equitable decision-making processes and the attractiveness of the solutions themselves.

f. Recognize that empowering people to equitably engage in solutions will be enormously aided by an increase in the ability to measure and publicize the immediate improvements in health and health savings that result from climate action.[89]

THE ACE NATIONAL FOCAL POINT SHOULD:

a. Establish and manage a long-term infrastructure to guide national-scale messaging priorities and develop simple and effective messages based on communication research.[90] The messaging infrastructure should include a range of ACE-relevant researchers and practitioners in order to guide deployment of effective messages.

b. Work with social science researchers to develop the metrics necessary to assess and track public understanding, values, perceptions, and attitudes about climate change over time.

c. Work with communication researchers and others in the ACE community to develop a coherent understanding of climate solutions.

d. Ensure that the public receives up-to-date and reliable information about climate risks and their causes, as well as information about the positive impacts of climate solutions.

e. Develop a publicly accessible dashboard of actions by the ACE community that includes factors such as the people reached, and actions people have taken as a result.

f. Seek additional dialogue with the ACE community to identify strategies to encourage climate-friendly lifestyles and behaviors and implement climate change policies.

4. *Public Access to Information Recommendations — "Public access to information strengthens connections between knowledge production, knowledge sharing and decision-making, and provides people with the tools they need to play an active role in addressing climate change."*[91]

THE ACE NATIONAL STRATEGY SHOULD:

a. Establish lasting protocols to ensure public access to information about climate research, solutions, and decision-making. Such protocols should enshrine public access to government-generated data and information and promote public access to information held by non-governmental organizations, businesses, and local communities.

b. Establish protocols with Tribal Nations for respectful sharing and public access to information about climate research, solutions, and decision-making.

c. Incentivize or require the sharing of climate-relevant knowledge in federal contracting and procurement policies.

d. Incentivize the sharing of the data, models, and other information resources that are needed to empower concerted action across various professions and localities. The strategy should align with existing models, such as the Urban Climate Change Research Network, the Urban Sustainability Directors Network, the Association of Climate Change Officers, CoolCalifornia.org, UNESCO Climate Frontlines, and many others.

e. Treat the Internet as a public utility, develop policies to ensure equitable access, and reduce barriers to education and workforce training.

THE ACE NATIONAL FOCAL POINT SHOULD:

a. Develop and manage protocols and platforms that encourage efficient knowledge sharing among diverse local communities and ACE practitioners in various professions.

5. *Public Participation Recommendations — "Public participation ensures ownership by encouraging people to be more attentive to policy-making and participate in the implementation of climate policies."*[92]

THE ACE NATIONAL STRATEGY SHOULD:

a. Prioritize the training of policymakers, executives, and senior decision-makers in philanthropic institutions in processes that encourage inclusive public participation and are responsive to the social, economic, geographical, and gender characteristics of the communities they serve.
b. Develop and deploy infrastructure to encourage and support ongoing trust-building community-level dialogues equivalent to the U.N. Talanoa Dialogue Platform. This includes establishing protocols for municipal decision-making that create space for public dialogue about climate action plans.
c. Establish additional processes that promote and enable public participation in decision-making.
d. Prioritize a shift away from an information-gathering model in decision-making to the implementation of a consent model in order to ensure that the concerns of marginalized peoples are genuinely addressed.
e. Require that policymaking at all levels of government be informed by Indigenous Peoples' input, practices, and ways of knowing so that their ways of life are protected.

f. Prioritize a shift from net-zero approaches to greenhouse gas mitigation to zero-emissions approaches in order to avoid further degradation of natural ecosystems and human health. ACE community members note that a net-zero approach allows for the continuation of pollution that disproportionally harms the health of BIPOC and low-income communities.

THE ACE NATIONAL FOCAL POINT SHOULD:

a. Work with national and state legislatures to build equitable public participation into climate-related legislation.

6. *Coordination and Collaboration Recommendations — "These five elements can all be strengthened through international cooperation. Governments and organizations can support each other with resources, technical expertise, ideas and inspiration for developing climate action programmes."*[93]

THE ACE NATIONAL STRATEGY SHOULD:

a. Re-commit to the UNFCCC and the Paris Agreement with increasingly ambitious goals for rapid decarbonization of the economy and the protection of the nation's most vulnerable peoples and natural systems.
b. Be integrated into the U.S. 2020 Nationally Determined Contribution to the UNFCCC process.
c. Clearly articulate how the ACE agenda will accelerate a just transition to a low-carbon world.
d. Designate the U.S. ACE National Focal Point and articulate its operational framework, including a diverse staff and embrace of a distributed network model for diverse and collaborative leadership.

e. Provide long-term authority to, and financial support for, NFP operations.

f. Require every federal agency to develop a climate action plan that incorporates and operationalizes ACE strategies.

g. While not mentioned in the dialogues, the national strategy should ensure that international cooperation aligns with a justice agenda.[94]

THE ACE NATIONAL FOCAL POINT SHOULD:

a. Establish protocols and infrastructure for periodic assessments of public knowledge, perceptions, and attitudes about climate change, as noted earlier. These assessments should be reported to the public and to the UNFCCC on a regular basis. At a minimum, reporting should be included in subsequent NDCs.

b. Embrace and meet its obligations to collaborate at the international level, share knowledge, and bring international knowledge to the ACE community in the U.S.

c. Work with Tribal Nations to build trust and set aside colonial thinking and practices in intergovernmental relationships.

d. Create a government cross-agency dashboard to measure progress on ACE implementation plans.

e. Foster cross-agency collaboration and knowledge sharing to improve ACE implementation.

f. Use its national coordination capacity to reduce duplication of effort, promote a shared vision, share best practices, guide investments strategically, and identify and fill gaps in ACE activities.

g. Promote climate solutions as a core activity for businesses, governments, and non-governmental organizations through regular meetings among senior leadership and governing boards.

VIII. The Path Forward

The ACE community calls upon the United States to insert the following language, or its equivalent, into the 2020 Nationally Determined Contribution:

> The United States commits to nominate a National Focal Point for Action for Climate Empowerment (ACE) and establish a diverse ACE Task Team that will utilize the community-developed *An ACE National Strategic Planning Framework for the United States* to create an ACE national strategy for delivery at COP26 and follow through on its implementation.

This *Strategic Planning Framework* lays the foundation for this crucial work. Adding such language to the 2020 NDC will commit the nation to building upon the contributions of the ACE community through a fast-paced, inclusive, multi-sectoral, and participatory process that reflects the U.S. national circumstances and the priorities and wisdom of the nation's leaders in education and public empowerment, civic engagement, climate justice, and climate solutions. The ACE community recognizes that respectful relationships with Tribal Nations are critical to this process. Members of the ACE community are ready to assist and support the development and implementation of an ACE national strategic plan for the United States in 2021.

Time is of the essence. The urgency of this work is evident in the rapidly changing climate system, rising concentrations of greenhouse gases in the atmosphere, negative impacts on communities and public health, and the degradation and loss of natural ecosystems. National commitments to the UNFCCC treaty and its processes further demand that the United States act quickly, decisively, and skillfully in meeting the Action for Climate Empowerment mandates and recommendations.

UNESCO/UNFCCC Secretariat guidelines call upon national governments to establish, fund, and empower the NFP and an

ACE Task Team typically comprising "five to ten investigators/ consultants with broad knowledge across the six ACE elements who are able to invest significant time and energy to support and develop the National ACE Strategy."[95] Members of the Task Team must have deep and broad knowledge and experience in ACE disciplines and fields of practice. The guidelines and the ACE community call for the ACE Task Team to reflect gender and BIPOC diversity in addition to professional expertise.

UNESCO/UNFCCC Secretariat guidelines call for the Task Team to begin the strategic planning process with "a desktop review of existing ACE policies and initiatives and by conducting a stakeholder mapping exercise...leading to the creation of a background document synthesizing all of the findings."[96] While this *Strategic Planning Framework* does not provide the necessary policy survey, it makes significant contributions by engaging ACE stakeholders and actors in the United States and providing the initial stakeholder map and background synthesis. We urge the NFP to expand on this work by organizing additional multi-sectoral Talanoa-style dialogues in order to flesh out these findings with additional insights from national and sub-national governments, BIPOC, rural communities, community groups, behavioral scientists, climate scientists, educators, media and communicators, health organizations, labor groups, publicly- and privately-held businesses, and others.

Moreover, the ACE community calls upon the United States to empower the NFP and its staff as a long-term, proactive, multi-faceted, and entrepreneurial enterprise that seeks expertise and input from diverse stakeholders frequently, assesses progress regularly, and guides the implementation of the national strategy through active engagement and support.

By delivering an ACE national strategy at COP26, the United States will become the first major emitting country to do so. But delivering the strategy is the beginning, not the end, of this all-important process. A national strategy that is co-developed with and by the diverse members of the ACE community will overcome a crucial obstacle in meeting the climate crisis. The national strategy will, at last, give coherence to the nation's diverse and inspiring efforts, and thereby empower the nation to make rapid and robust progress in solving the climate crisis.

Chapter 5

Commentaries

Education Is Essential to Achieving Our Climate Goals
Judy Braus, Brock Adler, and Sarah Bodor
North American Association for Environmental Education
(NAAEE)

An ACE National Strategic Framework for the United States presents an unprecedented opportunity for government agencies, non-profit organizations, and the philanthropic community to embrace the critical role of climate change education and civic engagement in our nation's effort to advance climate solutions. The environmental education community has long prioritized climate change education—from compiling and disseminating research about what works in climate change education to advancing policies that bring in more support and funding to creative programming and professional development in both the formal and informal sectors.

What's needed now is a determined effort to expand teaching climate change science into an interdisciplinary and cross-sector approach for all ages. Education is essential to building more resilient communities, developing a climate-savvy workforce, and aligning and scaling our efforts to create a civically engaged citizenry. In schools, for example, civics education, much like environmental education, has been seriously underfunded. Many high-school graduates don't understand how to get engaged in civic life—individually or collectively. We need to advance climate change policy at the local, state, and national levels. We need to work across the country and collaboratively with colleagues to fund and support climate change learning. This is exactly what the ACE process promises.

Environmental education focuses on lifelong learning to promote the knowledge, skills, and dispositions that lead to being active in civic life. We've also been focused on how we can create a more equitable and inclusive field and society. This aligns with the *Strategic Planning Framework*'s focus on climate justice and on local and Indigenous knowledge and insights.

The *Strategic Planning Framework* aligns with the ongoing work of NAAEE and the field and offers an opportunity for us to collaborate more effectively and build bridges across disciplines and sectors to accomplish more together to address the serious and growing threats from climate change. Achieving the vision in the framework requires us to work more collaboratively with our colleagues in the social sciences, communication, the sciences, urban planning, justice, and other fields to more fully create deep and lasting positive change.

We look forward to working with our existing and new international, national, state, and local partners to align our work and think more strategically, building on existing successes and models. We are excited to pursue new legislation that builds political will on all sides, and brings more organizations, agencies, and others into the fold. We hope that this framework allows others to take the lead on specific aspects of a national strategy. This will play to the strengths of the multiple organizations working in this space, including those advancing climate change education policy. Climate education is a major component of environmental education and, as such, we will use all that we've learned about what works in education to advance our efforts. Climate change is arguably the most complex and significant long-term threat facing our nation and our planet today. The framework's emphasis on climate empowerment and public participation presents an opportunity for all of us working in education to accomplish more together and achieve a greater impact.

ACE Turns Local Residents into Climate Leaders
Chris Castro
Director, Office of Sustainability & Resilience
City of Orlando, Florida

Working in local government, I've quickly come to realize the value of an educated, engaged, and empowered public that is looking to shape their community for the better. In Orlando, we have passed some of the most ambitious climate policies and programs in the country, most of which have been created with very strong public participation and support.

Community-based organizations and nonprofits are building coalitions to rally around local climate goal setting and policy making. They include the First 50 coalition in Orlando, which is made up of the local chapters of the NAACP, Sierra Club, League of Women Voters, IDEAS For Us, Solar United Neighbors, and others. There are over 50 members to date.

An ACE national strategy—especially one that emphasizes decision-making and actions in and by local communities—is an integral part of our journey for shaping the future that we want. Importantly, the *Strategic Planning Framework* truly embraces a linkage between social justice and climate action. These issues are inextricably linked and must be solved together.

We are demonstrating how the *Strategic Planning Framework's* approach to ACE works on the ground. One of the local community workshops in Orlando is known as the IDEAS Hive. It is a monthly think-tank that brings together people of all ages and all backgrounds. The workshops combine a TEDx-style lecture series with creative break-out sessions to stimulate ideation and invent solutions using human-centered design and biomimicry principles. These are like speakeasies for innovation. Ultimately, they help people co-create projects, initiatives, and campaigns that advance the United Nation's Sustainable Development Goals through community action. These events have become a "third-place" for public participation in our community that enables robust knowledge sharing and crowdsourcing of ideas.

In our experience, this is a recipe for community-led solutions to our local and global challenges. Community actions come from these workshop sessions: we have seen residents performing reforestation efforts, shoreline and wetland restorations, urban farming, solar panel installations, community composting, and dozens more projects. Between 2013 and 2020, the IDEAS Hive has been held over 100 times in Orlando, engaging thousands of residents in efforts to mold our local community's future. The participants have become leaders in sustainability and addressing the climate crisis. Many have also written emails to our elected officials, phone banked, and ultimately testified in City Council when we brought forward the ambitious climate and sustainability policies that will move us in the right direction.

A national strategy that empowers local residents to create solutions, act on them, and become leaders is a practical and effective model for overcoming the climate challenge.

Abe Lincoln Would Love this Initiative
Rob Gould, Ph.D.
Director of Strategic Communication
Medical Society Consortium on Climate & Health

Most know that Abraham Lincoln said "public sentiment is everything. With public sentiment, nothing can fail; without it nothing can succeed." Fewer know that he used this comment on the role of public engagement in political persuasion to attack William Douglas for shaping public sentiment to accept that new states might embrace slavery.

On the one hand, Lincoln knew public sentiment is determinative. On the other, he knew it was often much too easily swayed. Lincoln also knew that demagogues are less interested in responding to public sentiment than to shaping it toward their interests.

I point to this well-worn anecdote to say Lincoln would love *An ACE National Strategic Planning Framework of the United States.* He'd see it as I do: that public buy-in to climate solutions—and resistance to demagoguery—can only be achieved through true participation in the solution-generating process itself. The document, whose creation applied the same collaborative approach that it prescribes to ensure full-throated and informed public participation in the issue that will define the trajectory of our lives on this planet, has elevated "recommendations for a process to find the best solutions" to commanding equal stature with the solutions themselves.

Effective Climate Empowerment Requires a "Middle Out" Strategy
Edward Maibach, M.P.H. Ph.D.
Distinguished University Professor and Director
George Mason University Center for Climate Change
Communication

What is climate empowerment, and how can our nation rapidly achieve it? These are important questions that the authors of *ACE National Strategic Planning Framework for the United States* wrestled with—in my opinion intelligently, insightfully, and effectively.

Our federal government must play *a* leading role in driving and helping to fund America's climate empowerment process, but we won't make sufficient progress if it is playing *the* leading role. The process must be co-owned by stakeholders as diverse as the United States itself, including but not necessarily limited to states, cities and counties, civic organizations, professional societies, advocacy groups, Tribes and Indigenous organizations, and businesses large and small.

Diverse and decentralized ownership of the process is

necessary, in part, because the task at hand requires rethinking and resetting many of the assumptions that have guided the actions of all these stakeholders for the past several generations — based on the presumption of a stable climate. The other reason this process can't be led solely by the federal government is because — as we have seen clearly over the past several decades — the federal government can't be expected to lead unless an enduring coalition of the stakeholders demands that leadership.

A top-down strategy — even if conditions exist today for top-down leadership — is not likely to be enduring. A bottom-up strategy — where we (individuals and families, communities, businesses, and so on) are expected to figure it out and adapt accordingly — is doomed to fail for many reasons and in many ways. What's needed for climate empowerment is a robust "middle-out" strategy. By building an enduring coalition of stakeholders that are committed to fairly and effectively addressing climate change, we can accomplish two necessary objectives. First, we can sustain the necessary pressure on the federal government to enact the policies and to develop and support the programs that are needed — many of which have not yet been thought of or proposed. Second, we can create conditions and resources to enable all of the individuals, groups, and organizations mentioned above to participate effectively in the necessary bottom-up change process.

It's not clear that we currently know the best way to create such a middle-out strategy, but what's clear is that we should look to other highly effective national initiatives — here and abroad — for inspiration and guidance. The National High Blood Pressure Education Program — coordinated by the National Institutes of Health, but co-created and co-owned by health voluntary associations, health professional organizations, patient advocacy groups, civil rights organizations, the pharmaceutical industry, and others — is one possible example. Where are the others, and what are their lessons for meeting our current challenge?

An ACE Strategy Must Be Prepared for Opposition
Bill McKibben
Author of *Falter: Has the Human Game Begun to Play Itself Out?*

This ACE Framework makes obvious sense—it's the kind of straightforward task the U.S. and all other nations should have engaged in 30 years ago. That we didn't do so was not due to oversight, however—as we now know from great investigative reporting, it was a conscious decision by many of the players in this fight. The fossil fuel industry is less strong than they were a decade ago, but they retain the political power necessary to scuttle attempts at quick remediation of climate change. And so planning for this kind of effort needs to be undertaken in the knowledge that it will be opposed. That opposition need not be fatal: the fossil fuel industry is slowly losing the messaging war, as more and more people understand that renewable energy is affordable as well as clean. But fighting it effectively means, among other things, assuring those currently at work in coal, oil, and especially gas that there are in place plans that will allow for a fair transition to new work that helps the planet.

The Importance of this Genuine and Diverse Collaboration to Effectively Address the Climate Crisis
Sherri Mitchell—Weh'na Ha'mu Kwasset of the Penobscot Nation, J.D.

In the past six months, I have had the honor of coming together with a diverse group of representatives from across the United States to design *An ACE National Framework Strategy for the United States.* To my knowledge, this is the first time that such a diverse group of representatives have come together to openly discuss a unified strategy for the most pressing problem of our time, climate change. The significance of this collaboration cannot be overstated. It is likely the most promising strategy that we have for addressing the critical challenge that climate change presents.

In 1953, Felix Cohen, who was instrumental in shaping Federal Indian Law and Policy, said,

> Like the miner's canary, the Indian marks the shift from fresh air to poison gas in our political atmosphere; and our treatment of Indians, even more than our treatment of other minorities, reflects the rise and fall in our democratic faith.

For the past fifty years, American Indian Peoples have been on the front lines of environmental racism, with toxic industry placed along the border of our communities and directly through our waterways, causing myriad illnesses and health complications in our communities. We have also faced the earliest impacts of climate change with rising tides, hurricanes, and droughts that have caused wide-scale destruction of our territories. However, we are largely left out of the emerging conversations regarding the distribution of funding and other resources for climate change mitigation and adaptation. And, our free, prior, and informed consent is almost never sought when green-washed climate change "solutions" are put forth in our communities, such as hydroelectric dams, which often result in large-scale territorial loss for our Peoples.

Today, most remaining untouched lands on Mother Earth are in the hands of Indigenous Peoples. These lands are consistently under threat of loss, most often from irresponsible industrial expansion, but more and more those threats are coming from climate change measures that were decided upon without the consultation or ecological knowledge of the Indigenous Peoples who have lived in relationship with those lands for millennia. If we hope to address the ravishing impacts of climate change within the limited timeframe that we have, all voices need to be included, heeded, and integrated into the strategies that are being developed. The *ACE National Strategic Planning Framework* would allow us to activate people across the spectrum of human experience as co-creators of new policies, understandings, and behavioral norms, to rapidly and efficiently accelerate a transition to a low-carbon world that is equitable and just. My hope is that this process will lead to common sense, life-affirming choices that will allow this nation to step away from the edge of total environmental destruction and move expeditiously back into alignment with a sustainable future, for those here now and for the generations who will follow.

At the Intersection of Environmental Justice
Taylor Morton
WE ACT for Environmental Justice

When working at the intersection of education, environmental justice, and health, it has always been important to have a strong and comprehensive strategy at the national level. The ACE *Strategic Planning Framework* has gathered community members, health experts, climate scientists, and many other crucial parties to put equity and justice at the center of decision-making on climate, economy, education, COVID-19, and other natural interests.

The potential impact of this will be influential by building on actions that embody the fact that equity and justice are inseparable from climate and environmental work. Implementing a national strategy such as this will require close accountability from elected officials, and close engagement with historically under-resourced communities. The work that is done around environmental and climate justice is framed around meaningful involvement, fair treatment, and accountability. This must be the core of what we do as a nation; and is what the ACE national strategy strives to accomplish. Although these are difficult to implement at times, we owe it to the marginalized communities that support this nation to be as equitable and just as possible, especially around climate and environment.

Driving Corporate Climate Action from Within
Andrew Winston
Sustainability advisor and author of *The Big Pivot* and *Green to Gold*

The vast majority of the business world has stopped debating whether the climate crisis is a serious issue. More than 90 percent of the world's largest companies have set public targets to reduce energy use or carbon emissions. For more than 1,000 companies, those goals commit them to reduce emissions at the pace that science says is necessary (so-called science-based targets). And yet, corporate action in total is not remotely enough. The world is not on a path to slow climate change to 2°C warming, let alone the 1.5°C needed to save low-lying areas and avoid catastrophic outcomes.

Companies need to move faster, and pressure from key stakeholders can help motivate them. Three groups have the best chance of shifting corporate behavior: investors, consumers, and employees. Investors as an institution have long been a hindrance to climate action—they have seen it as detrimental to profits—but are starting to come around. Consumers and employees are, of course, just people and part of the public at large. The U.N.'s ACE agenda will reach and activate people who, as consumers and employees, can make it clear that they want companies to scale up their climate efforts.

The group that has the most momentum and potential is employees. Companies need to attract and retain talent, and the younger Millennial and Gen Z workers—making up more than half the workforce—want action on sustainability and climate change. More than half of Millennials say they have already ruled out working for a company because of its values. And 90 percent of Gen Zers think companies have an obligation to solve environmental social problems.[1]

Employees, particularly in the tech sector, are already a force for change. In 2019, nearly 9,000 Amazon employees wrote an open letter to CEO Jeff Bezos demanding that the company set science-based carbon reduction targets and stop donating to politicians that deny climate change. The company, after years of mostly silence on the issue, set some of the most aggressive targets in the world, including carbon neutrality by 2040. Google and Microsoft employees have taken similar measures and even staged a walkout for global climate marches.

Stakeholder pressure is critical for speeding up climate action. Many companies want to go faster but worry it will cost too much and displease investors (in fact, most of the actions companies take to reduce emissions save money—renewable energy is cheaper than fossil fuels, for example). But there is fear of how investors will react, and top executives will say, "I'd like to do more, but my shareholders..." Real pressure from employees and the public can provide cover for setting bigger goals and making the necessary investments in carbon reduction and climate justice.

People have enormous power as employees, consumers, and even as investors—they can direct their savings to sustainable investing options. If a large percentage of the public is inspired to use that power and demand action from all institutions, watch out.

Chapter 6

Lessons for the Future of Climate Empowerment

The processes that produced the *Strategic Planning Framework* provide some important reminders about the ways in which people think about and solve complex problems together. Those processes brought a very diverse group of people together around a very specific goal, namely, to develop a coherent, overarching national strategy that will inform—and probably transform—the ways in which all of the participants do their work.

Many of the participants share similar challenges, including a shortage of adequate and sustained funding, difficulties gaining access to the places where ACE implementation decisions are often made, and the lack of an expressed commitment by national political and corporate leaders to prioritize climate action in the nation's political life. The participants' widespread experiences with these challenges certainly helped them empathize and find common purpose with their peers.

There is another characteristic, as well, that should not be overlooked: the development of *An ACE National Strategic Planning Framework for the United States* was an entrepreneurial enterprise. No national mandate or institutional requirement led to its creation. Nobody's job description included "develop a national strategy for ACE." Those who chose to participate did so with the understanding that any benefits flowing from this project would need to be of their own making. The fact that so many people accepted this challenge is no accident. Given the many obstacles facing everyone who takes this work seriously in the United States, an entrepreneurial spirit is, more or less, required. That spirit is evident throughout the *Strategic Planning*

Framework, just as it was evident in the ways in which people went about planning and executing the work.

As we consider expanding on this pilot project in the United States, we are aware that preserving this entrepreneurial spirit will be crucial. Strategic planning can easily devolve into a formal procedure that delivers a lifeless product. But when people are fully committed to a goal of great importance, their collaboration is enlivened and the strategy can flow almost seamlessly into implementation. The "how" and "who" are just as important as the "what." Making smart choices about all three elements is critical to a successful outcome that takes on a life of its own.

ACE practitioners in the United States have provided insights into the ways in which people and societies can change when necessary. Chief among these is the insight that people learn everywhere, in every context, and in multiple ways. Sometimes, people adopt new behaviors in response to learning something new. At other times, people's knowledge and understanding evolves in response to their having adopted new behaviors. These processes are multi-faceted and non-linear. People perceive their world and make sense of their circumstances emotionally, as well as conceptually. We learn in relationship with others, with the places we inhabit and visit, and through the activities of everyday life.

One of the most significant decisions made in planning for the Talanoa-style dialogues in August of 2020 was the decision to stretch the cross-sectoral structure of ACE even further than the UNESCO/UNFCCC Secretariat guidelines suggested. ACE identifies six different elements that have overlapping objectives: education, training, public awareness, public access to information, public participation, and international cooperation. The *Strategic Planning Framework* coordinating team recognized the dangers inherent in allowing educators to collaborate on the first element, communication professionals and social marketers to work only on the third, and so forth. The genius of the ACE elements is, in fact, that professions cannot be slotted neatly into just one of the elements. The coordinating team, therefore, decided to organize four online dialogue sessions rather than six. Structuring the process this way strongly encouraged educators, social marketers, activists, policymakers, and others to confront a wide range of challenges and opportunities together. This decision to intentionally cross-pollinate typically siloed areas encouraged collaboration on a national strategy in unexpected ways and with people we did not previously know.

We hope that anyone who undertakes a national strategic planning process for ACE will see the value in approaching the task this way. Competition for resources, attention, theories of change, or overall "ownership" of the issue has a polarizing effect that can hinder the ACE community's climate action and climate justice work overall. The *Strategic Planning Framework* clearly states the vital importance of just and equitable processes. We hasten to stress that the outcome of this project is a substantive document precisely because the coordinating team understood the importance of working across boundaries, values systems, and professional norms. Entrepreneurship is about putting familiar pieces together in unexpected ways to create something valuable and new. As BIPOC participants noted, this includes histories that have been erased, and knowledge and practices that have typically been excluded. Failing to embrace this approach, both in spirit and in practical decision-making, would undermine the transformative potential that the strategic planning process is capable of achieving.

Finally, because we were uniquely positioned as inside observers throughout this entire project, we call attention to the importance of building upon trusted relationships between people and networks. As noted in the first chapter of this book, ACE strategic planning could easily be assigned to one or several federal agencies or to a multi-agency working group. Completing a U.S. ACE national strategy might, in fact, be accomplished using such a structure. The organizers of the *Strategic Planning Framework* did not have the authority to commission such a process. Instead, they drew upon their own personal and professional networks to build a multi-faceted coordinating team. Together, they used a network-of-networks approach to recruit a remarkably diverse and highly qualified group of people into the dialogue and review process. Participants opted in because they trusted that those who invited them would not waste their time. Conversely, the trust placed in the coordination team encouraged them to work hard not to let the participants down.

There is a vitality in any project that puts people's relationships and reputations on the line. Risk is part of every entrepreneurial initiative and, in our view, it was central to the success of this initiative. We doubt that a safer and more formal process would have met the spirit of the Action for Climate Empowerment vision and goals.

The *Resetting Our Future* book series was born out of the dark challenges of 2020: the COVID-19 pandemic, the economic crisis, and frequent police violence against Black Americans. The organizing idea is that people can use times of crisis to reassess our collective circumstances and address some of society's greatest challenges in the recovery process. These include climate change, systemic racism and injustice against BIPOC, the marginalization of low-income communities, gaps in education and equitable access to learning and career training, and so forth.

Those who undertook *An ACE National Strategic Planning Framework for the United States* embodied this same spirit. They did not sit back and wait for the government to produce a national strategy, nor did they limit the focus to one small aspect of the six ACE elements. Instead, they sought to create an open and wide-ranging dialogue process that treated everyone equitably and with respect. This allowed everyone to see the intersections between these vexing societal challenges and co-create a platform that can help us alleviate a number of challenges all at once. Open-ended and trusting processes are, in fact, how groups of people discover the cruxes of the issues together. We are inspired by what has been accomplished here and by the opportunities that this pilot project presents as humanity confronts a better future together.

Editor Biographies

Deb Morrison, Ph.D.

Dr. Deb Morrison served as Strategic Designer and Writing Team Co-lead for the U.S. Action for Climate Empowerment Strategic Planning Framework. Deb has been involved in climate and justice learning design as a researcher-practice partner with numerous communities, and as an implementer of systemic change. She is part of the leadership team designing and implementing the ClimeTime initiative in Washington State, is a board member of the Climate Literacy and Energy Awareness Network (CLEAN), and is involved in designing and implementing the research-practice partnership for Advancing Coherent and Equitable Systems of Science Education. Deb co-chairs the National Association of Research in Science Teaching (NARST) policy and programs committee, serves on the steering committee for the UNFCCC ECOS community, and sits on the TETÁĆES Climate Action Steering Committee. She is the author of numerous book chapters and articles on education, justice in the sciences, and justice in science education.

Follow Deb Morrison at:
www.debmorrison.me
www.facebook.com/educatordeb
@educatordeb

Tom Bowman

Tom Bowman served as Strategic Advisor and Writing Team Co-lead for the U.S. Action for Climate Empowerment Strategic Planning Framework. The Framework is an initiative by social scientists, educators, scientists, and activists to help the United States meet and exceed the goals of the Paris Agreement. Tom founded Bowman Design Group and Bowman Change, Inc., a strategic communication consultancy. He works with federal agencies, corporate leadership, entrepreneurs, and leading cultural institutions such as NOAA, NASA, the National Academy of Sciences and the Aquarium of the Pacific. Tom's company received a Cool California Small Business of the Year Award for decarbonizing business operations. His work received White House Champions of Change recognition, and he was inducted into the International Green Industry Hall of Fame. Tom is a popular public speaker and author of *Resetting Our Future: What if Solving the Climate Crisis Is Simple?* and *The Green Edge*.

Follow Tom Bowman at:
www.BowmanChange.com
www.facebook.com/BowmanClimate
@BowmanClimate

Follow the U.S. ACE Framework at:
www.aceframework.us

Appendix to Chapter 4

A: How the Strategic Planning Framework Was Created

The *Strategic Planning Framework* developed out of decades of thinking and work by ACE community members across the United States and began to coalesce more formally through a series of meetings and workshops in the past few years. More recently, in a 2019 conference workshop, participants explored ways to advance implementation of UNFCCC Article 6—Action for Climate Empowerment—in the United States. Participants concluded that the nation's highly diverse community of ACE organizations, networks, and individuals should undertake the development of a strategic planning framework in order to accelerate and inform creation of the first U.S. ACE national strategy.

Members of the Climate Literacy and Energy Awareness Network (CLEAN), which is a very active community of educators who share resources and advocate for climate education, took the idea to their leadership board. The board agreed in December 2019 and advised that a successful strategy development process should be accomplished by a very broad and diverse coalition of actors.

CLEAN undertook a series of monthly ACE listening sessions in order to provide input to the process. Meanwhile, members of CLEAN and the Climate Education, Communication, and Outreach Stakeholder Community (ECOS) assembled an 11-member coordinating team comprising experts from government, formal and informal education institutions, social movements, BIPOC, and the private sector. The team organized and facilitated a series of five online events: an orientation session with panels representing the diversity of the ACE community, plus four, three-hour long, multi-sector dialogues based on the U.N. Talanoa Dialogue Platform. The spirit of the Talanoa process is to create inclusive stakeholder-facilitated meetings in which all participants are considered peers regardless of position or influence. These sessions were conducted in August of 2020 and took place online due to the COVID-19 pandemic.

Each dialogue featured a back-casting approach developed by the Citizens' Climate Engagement Network in its Engage4Climate toolkit.[97] The back-casting process saw participants describing what an empowered, informed, and active society would look like in 2040, and then recommending specific actions that are needed in order to achieve the result in ten-, five-, and two-year timeframes.

Dialogue facilitators and rapporteurs recorded the ACE community's inputs. A small team of writers synthesized the notes and drafted the *Strategic Planning Framework* for community review. The review was conducted in three steps: (1) by the coordinating team, (2) by a select group of strategic reviewers who were invited for their expertise and leadership in various aspects of ACE, and (3) finally by the dialogue participants and the larger ACE community in the United States. *An ACE National Strategic Planning Framework for the United States* is the result of the ACE community's collective work.

Participants, Shapers, and Contributors

Participation in this community-driven initiative was entirely voluntary. Nevertheless, 150 individuals from 120 different organizations and networks provided substantive contributions to the process through the dialogues and reviews. A voluntary survey of dialogue participants demonstrates the diversity that this pilot project achieved:

- Gender diversity: 68% female, 30% male, 1% non-binary, 1% preferred not to say
- Ethnic diversity: 68.5% white, 11.8% Hispanic or Latinx, 7.9% Asian American, 7.9% Black or African American,

3.1% American Indian or Alaska Native, 0.8% Native Hawaiian or Other Pacific Islander

- From predominantly BIPOC communities: 31.6% yes, 68.4% no
- From predominantly low-income communities: 35.9% yes, 64.1% no
- Age diversity: 9.4% 18–24, 18.8% 25–34, 27.4% 35–44, 14.5% 45–54, 19.7% 55–64, 9.4% 65–74, 0.9% 75–84

Professional Affiliations of the Participants, Shapers, and Contributors

Alliance for Climate Education

America Adapts Media

American Society of Adaptation Professionals

AMS Education Program

Aquarium of the Pacific

Arizona State University

Blue Sky Funders Forum

Bowman Change, Inc.

Braided Education Consulting

Capital District Regional Planning Commission

Carleton College

Center for New Meaning

Central Community College

Changemakers Books

Chrysalis Management Services

Citizens' Climate Lobby

City of Orlando

City of San Luis Obispo

CIVICUS

Clark Atlanta University

Climate Access

Climate Central

Climate Generation: A Will Steger Legacy

Climate Literacy and Energy Awareness Network

Climate Resilience Solutions, LLC

Climate Voice

CollabraLink, NOAA CPO

Colorado State University

Colorado University, Boulder

Columbia University

Communitopia

Cooperative Institute for Research in Environmental Sciences, CU Boulder

Cornell Community and Regional Development Institute

Cornell Cooperative Extension, Sullivan County

Cornell University

Cumberland River Compact

Ecology and Environment, Inc.

Eisele Architects

El Puente Latino Climate Action Network

El Yunque National Forest (USFS)

Environmental Finance Center

Environmental Students Leadership Initiative

Fenton

Finger Lakes Institute, Hobart and William Smith Colleges

Florida A&M University

Florida Sea Grant

Fond du Lac Tribal and Community College

Force of Nature

George Mason University

Global Youth Development Institute

Graduate School of Planning, University of Puerto Rico

Greater Portland Sustainability Education Network

Green Schools National Network, Inc.

Green the Church

HASKELL Indian Nations University

Hatch

Hazon

Historically Black Colleges and Universities Green Fund Inc.

Indigenous Environmental Network

Inside the Greenhouse

Insight Civil

Kinetic Communities Consulting

Knology

Livelihoods Knowledge Exchange Network

Local Government Commission

Mass Audubon

Member of the Royal Architectural Institute of Canada

Metropolitan Mayors Caucus

MI EGLE

Mississippi State University

Montana State University

National Aquarium

National Network for Ocean and Climate Change Interpretation

National Science Foundation, International

National Wildlife Federation

NEMAC+FernLeaf

New England Aquarium

New Hampshire Sea Grant Extension

New Jersey Department of Environmental Protection

New Mexico State University Cooperative Extension

New York City Dept. of Education, Office of Sustainability

New York City Dept. of Environmental Conservation, Office of
    Climate Change

New York City Mayor's Office

New York State Energy Research and Development Authority

NOAA Chesapeake Bay Office

NOAA Climate Program Office

NOAA Education

NOAA Fisheries

NOAA Office of Education Northern Gulf of Mexico Sentinel

Site Cooperative
NOAA NWS Caribbean Tsunami Warning Program
North American Association for Environmental Education
North Carolina Cooperative Extension
Northwestern University
Nuclear New York
Ohio University & Desert Research Institute
Oregon State University
Paul Smith's College of the Adirondacks
Portland State University
Project Drawdown
Puerto Rico Climate Change Council
Puerto Rico Dept. of Natural Resources, Office for Coastal Management and Climate Change
Puerto Rico Science, Technology and Research Trust
Renewable Energy Alaska Project
Sea Grant Puerto Rico
Second Nature
Sociedad Ambiente Marino
Solstice Initiative, Inc.
South Louisiana Wetlands Discovery Center
Spokane Tribe of the Spokane Reservation
Stanford University
State of California Ten Strands
Terra.do
The Aspen Institute
The Brookings Institution
The CLEO Institute
The Franklin Institute
The Great Plains Institute
The Harbinger Consulting Group
The Mara Partners
The Wild Center
UCAR Center for Science Education

U-Hope Consulting, LLC

United Nations Climate Education, Communication, and Outreach Stakeholders (ECOS)

United Nations Framework Convention on Climate Change (UNFCCC)

University of California, Berkeley

University of California, Irvine

University of California, Merced

University of California Agriculture and Natural Resources

University of California Cooperative Extension/California Naturalist

University of Colorado, Boulder

University of Florida, IFAS Extension

University of Maryland Extension

University of Massachusetts, Amherst

University of Nebraska, Lincoln School of Natural Resources

University of Puerto Rico, Río Piedras Campus

University of Rhode Island

University of San Diego

University of Washington

University of Wisconsin, Madison Extension

Urban Intersect Consulting

U.S. Department of State

U.S. Partnership for Education for Sustainable Development

Ward Museum, Salisbury University

Washington, D.C. Department of Energy and Environment

Washington State Department of Ecology

WE ACT for Environmental Justice

We Are Still In

Wisconsin Sea Grant

Yale Program on Climate Change Communication

Yale School of Forestry and Environmental Studies

Zoo Atlanta

Coordinating Team

Rebecca Anderson, Alliance for Climate Education

Tom Bowman, Bowman Change, Inc.

Isatis Cintrón Rodríguez, NSF GRFP and Citizens' Climate Lobby

Haley Crim, Village of Park Forest and Greenest Region Compact, and CLEAN Network

Timothy Damon, Global Youth Development Institute and Climate ECOS

Cyane Dandridge, Strategic Energy Innovations and School of Environmental Leadership

Hernán Gallo-Cornejo, Strategic Energy Innovations

Jen Kretser, The Wild Center

Deb Morrison, Ph.D. University of Washington

Frank Niepold, NOAA Climate Program Office and CLEAN Network

Kristen Poppleton, Climate Generation: A Will Steger Legacy

Billy Spitzer, Ph.D. National Network for Ocean and Climate Change Interpretation

Laura Weiland, Climate ECOS

Facilitators and Rapporteurs

Reginald Archer

Jack Barker

Ben Bronstein

Taylor Campbell-Mosley

Patrick Chandler

Isatis Cintron

John Coggin

Emily Courtney

Felicia Davis

Kali DeMarco

Thomas Di Liberto

Liam Engel

Liz Fitzpatrick
Monica Flores
Hernan Gallo
Ned Gardiner
Erin Glocke
Erin Griffin
Solemi Hernandez
Maxine Jimenez
Jen Kretser
Rohi Muthyala
Katya Obrez
Margaret Orr
Mildred Pierce
Billy Spitzer
Kamya Sud
Princella Talley
Tyler Valdes
Cheryl Watson
Laura Weiland

Writing Team
Tom Bowman, Bowman Change, Inc.
Deb Morrison, Ph.D. University of Washington

Strategic Reviewers
Elizabeth Bagley, Ph.D. Project Drawdown
Megan Bang, Northwestern University
Devarati Bhattacharya, Ph.D. University of Nebraska, Lincoln
Chris Castro, City of Orlando
Felicia Davis, Clark Atlanta University and HBCU Green Fund
Cristin Dorgelo, Association of Science-Technology Centers
Baruch Fischhoff, Ph.D. Carnegie Mellon University
Hernan Gallo, Strategic Energy Innovations
Robert Gould, Ph.D. One Degree Strategies

David Herring, NOAA Climate Program Office
Aryaana Khan, Alliance for Climate Education
Christina Kwauk, Brookings Institution
Anthony Leiserowitz, Ph.D. Yale University
Edward Maibach, Ph.D. George Mason University
Sherri Mitchell, JD, Indigenous Rights Attorney and Author
Taylor Morton, WE ACT for Environmental Justice
Cara Pike, Climate Access
Gail Scowcroft, Ph.D. University of Rhode Island and Climate
    Change Education Partners Alliance
Billy Spitzer, National Network for Ocean and Climate Change
    Interpretation
Daniel Wildcat, Ph.D. Haskell Indian Nations University

This document is not an official U.S. government product, nor is it reflective of official U.S. government policy. This is the product of a multi-stakeholder process of civil society.

Financial and Value in Kind Support

Bowman Change, Inc.
Citizens' Climate Lobby
Climate Education, Communication and Outreach Stakeholder
    Community
Climate Literacy and Energy Awareness Network
National Oceanic and Atmospheric Administration
Spencer Foundation
The Wild Center

An ACE National Strategic Planning Framework for the United States was prepared by the Bowman Change, Inc. under the contract WC-133R-14-BA-0026/1305M319FNRTMT1083 from the Climate Program Office's Communication, Education and Engagement Division of the National Oceanic and Atmospheric Administration (NOAA), U.S. Department of Commerce.

The statements, findings, conclusions, and recommendations are those of the author(s), dialogue and review participants and do not necessarily reflect the views of NOAA or the U.S. Department of Commerce.

This material is based upon work supported by the Spencer Foundation under Grant No. (202100079). Any opinions, findings, and conclusions or recommendations expressed in this material are those of the author(s) and do not necessarily reflect the views of the Spencer Foundation.

Suggested Citation

Bowman, T., Morrison, D. (2020) *An ACE National Strategic Planning Framework for the United States* [Online]. Created in collaborative reflection with the U.S. ACE Community. Available at http://aceframework.us.

B: Timeline of ACE Work in the United States

Please visit aceframework.us

References

Chapter 1: Welcome to the Strategic Planning Framework

1. See United Nations (2015) *Paris Agreement, Article 12*, p. 10: "Parties shall cooperate in taking measures, as appropriate, to enhance climate change education, training, public awareness, public participation and public access to information, recognizing the importance of these steps with respect to enhancing actions under this agreement."

2. See, for example: Oreskes, N. and Conway, E. M. (2010) *Merchants of Doubt*, New York, NY: Bloomsbury Press. See also: Mann, M. E. (2012) *The Hockey Stick and the Climate Wars: Dispatches from the Front Lines*, New York, NY: Columbia University Press.

3. Anonymous (2020) Unpublished dialogue, conducted by ACE Strategic Planning Framework coordinating team [Online], 13 August.

4. Yankelovich, D. (1999) *The Magic of Dialogue*, New York, NY: Touchstone, p. 17.

5. United Nations Climate Change (2018) *2018 Talanoa Dialogue Platform* [Online]. Available at https://unfccc. int/process-and-meetings/the-paris-agreement/the-paris-agreement/2018-talanoa-dialogue-platform.

6. Anonymous (2020) Email to Bowman, T., 23 August.

Chapter 2: Discoveries and Assumptions

1. Leiserowitz, A., Maibach, E., Rosenthal, S., Kotcher, J., Berquist, P., Ballew, M., Goldberg, M., Gustafson, A., Wang, X. (2020) *Climate Change in the American Mind: April 2020* [Online]. New Haven, CT: Yale Program on Climate Change Communication, p. 4. Available at: https:// climatecommunication.yale.edu/publications/climate-

111

change-in-the-american-mind-april-2020/.

2. Paas, L. and Goodman, D. (2016) *Action for Climate Empowerment: Guidelines for Accelerating Solutions through Education, Training and Public Awareness* [Online]. Paris and Bonn: United Nations Educational, Scientific and Cultural Organization and the Secretariat of the United Nations Convention on Climate Change, p. 14. Available at https://unfccc.int/files/cooperation_and_support/education_and_outreach/application/pdf/action_for_climate_empowerment_guidelines.pdf.

3. See: Executive Summary.

4. Anonymous (2020) Unpublished dialogue, conducted by ACE Strategic Planning Framework coordinating team [Online], 13 August.

Chapter 3: Engaging with Additional Dialogue Partners

1. Hultman, N., Frisch, C., Clark, L., Kennedy, K., Bodnar, P., Hansel, P., Cyrus, T., Manion, M., Edwards, M., Lund, J., Bowman, C., Jaeger, J., Cui, R., Clapper, A., Sen, A., Sha, D., Westphal, M., Jaglom, W., Altamirano, J. C., Hashimoto, H., Dennis, M., Hammound, K., Henderson, C., Zwicker, G., Ryan, M., O'Neill, J., Goldfield, E. (2019) *Accelerating America's Climate Pledge: Going All In to Build a Prosperous, Low-Carbon Economy for the United States* [Online]. Bloomberg Philanthropies, Rocky Mountain Institute, and World Resources Institute. New York, NY: Bloomberg Philanthropies, p. i. Available at https://assets.bbhub.io/dotorg/sites/28/2019/12/Accelerating-Americas-Pledge.pdf.

2. Hultman, N., et al. (2019), p. 2.

3. Hultman, N., et al. (2019), p. 7.

4. See, for example: Leiserowitz, A., Maibach, E., Roser-Renouf, C. (2009) *Global Warming's Six Americas 2009* [Online]. New Haven, CT: Yale Program on Climate Change

Communication. Available at https://climatecommunication.
yale.edu/publications/global-warmings-six-americas-2009/.

5. Marlon, J., Howe, P., Mildenberger, M., Leiserowitz, A.,
    Wang, X. (2020) *Yale Climate Opinion Maps 2020* [Online].
    New Haven, CT: Yale Program on Climate Change
    Communication. Available at https://climatecommunication.
    yale.edu/visualizations-data/ycom-us/.

6. Pilkington, E. (2017) 'Hookworm, a disease of extreme
    poverty, is thriving in the U.S. South. Why?', *The Guardian*,
    10 July [Online]. Available at https://www.theguardian.com/
    us-news/2017/sep/05/hookworm-lowndes-county-alabama-
    water-waste-treatment-poverty.

7. Del Real, J. A. (2019) 'How racism ripples through rural
    California's pipes', *The New York Times*, 29 November
    [Online]. Available at https://www.nytimes.com/2019/11/29/
    us/water-racism-california.html.

8. Dore, J. (2019) *Small Businesses Generate 44 Percent of U.S.
    Economic Activity*, 30 January [Online]. Washington, DC:
    U.S. Small Business Administration. Available at https://
    advocacy.sba.gov/2019/01/30/small-businesses-generate-44-
    percent-of-u-s-economic-activity/.

9. Fink, L. (2020) *A Fundamental Reshaping of Finance* [Online].
    New York, NY: BlackRock. Available at https://www.
    blackrock.com/corporate/investor-relations/larry-fink-ceo-
    letter.

Chapter 4: An ACE National Strategic Planning Framework for the United States

1. There are many government resources available covering
    climate science, evidence of change, and tools for climate
    action and increasing resilience. See, for example: www.
    climate.gov, the U.S. Climate Resilience Toolkit (https://
    toolkit.climate.gov), and many others.

2. Hultman, N., Frisch, C., Clark, L., Kennedy, K., Bodnar, P.,

Hansel, P., Cyrus, T., Manion, M., Edwards, M., Lund, J., Bowman, C., Jaeger, J., Cui, R., Clapper, A., Sen, A., Sha, D., Westphal, M., Jaglom, W., Altamirano, J. C., Hashimoto, H., Dennis, M., Hammound, K., Henderson, C., Zwicker, G., Ryan, M., O'Neill, J., Goldfield, E. (2019) *Accelerating America's Climate Pledge: Going All In to Build a Prosperous, Low-Carbon Economy for the United States* [Online]. Bloomberg Philanthropies, Rocky Mountain Institute, and World Resources Institute. New York, NY: Bloomberg Philanthropies, p. 2. Available at https://assets.bbhub.io/dotorg/sites/28/2019/12/Accelerating-Americas-Pledge.pdf.

3. See, for example: Kiem, A. S., Austin, E. K. (2013) 'Disconnect between science and end-users as a barrier to climate change adaptation', *Climate Research*, vol. 58, no. 1, pp. 29–41.

4. Leiserowitz, A., Maibach, E., Roser-Reneuf, C., Rosenthal, S., Cutler, M., Kotcher, J. (2018) *Climate Change in the American Mind: March 2018* [Online]. Yale University and George Mason University. New Haven, CT: Yale Program on Climate Change Communication. Available at https://climatecommunication.yale.edu/publications/climate-change-american-mind-march-2018

5. Goldberg, M., Gustafson, A., Rosenthal, S., Kotcher, J., Maibach, E., Leiserowitz, A. (2020) *For the First Time, the Alarmed Are Now the Largest of Global Warming's Six Americas* [Online]. Yale University and George Mason University. New Haven, CT: Yale Program on Climate Change Communication. Available at https://climatecommunication.yale.edu/publications/for-the-first-time-the-alarmed-are-now-the-largest-of-global-warmings-six-americas/.

6. Paas, L. and Goodman, D. (2016) *Action for Climate Empowerment: Guidelines for Accelerating Solutions through Education, Training and Public Awareness* [Online]. Paris and Bonn: United Nations Educational, Scientific and Cultural Organization and the Secretariat of the United Nations

Convention on Climate Change, p. 2. Available at https://unfccc.int/files/cooperation_and_support/education_and_outreach/application/pdf/action_for_climate_empowerment_guidelines.pdf.

7. United Nations Framework Convention on Climate Change (2016) *Article 12, Paris Agreement* [Online]. Available at https://unfccc.int/sites/default/files/english_paris_agreement.pdf.

8. United Nations (2019) 'Action for climate empowerment finds strong support at COP25', *United Nations Climate Change*, 11 December [Online]. Available at https://unfccc.int/news/action-for-climate-empowerment-finds-strong-support-at-cop25.

9. Worland, J. (2019) 'Climate change has already increased global inequity. It will only get worse', *Time*, 22 April [Online]. Available at https://time.com/5575523/climate-change-inequality/.

10. United Nations Climate Change (2019) *High-level Event on Action for Climate Empowerment at COP 25* [Online]. Available at https://unfccc.int/topics/education-youth/events-meetings/ace-day-other-events-at-cops/high-level-event-on-action-for-climate-empowerment-at-cop-25.

11. Kamarck, E. (2019) 'The challenging politics of climate change', *Brookings Institution*, 23 September [Online]. Washington, DC: Brookings Institute. Available at https://www.brookings.edu/research/the-challenging-politics-of-climate-change/.

12. Leiserowitz, A., Maibach, E., Rosenthal, S., Kotcher, J., Ballew, M., Bergquist, P., Gustafson, A., Goldberg, M., Wang, X. (2020) *Politics & Global Warming: April 2020* [Online]. Yale University and George Mason University. New Haven, CT: Yale Program on Climate Change Communication. Available at https://www.climatechangecommunication.org/wp-content/uploads/2020/06/politics-global-warming-april-2020c.pdf.

13. See, for example: Oreskes, N. and Conway, E. M. (2010) *Merchants of Doubt*, New York, NY: Bloomsbury Press.

14. See Appendix B.

15. Paas and Goodman (2016), p. 8.

16. United Nations Education Sector (2020) *Integrating Action for Climate Empowerment into Nationally Determined Contributions*. Paris: United Nations Educational, Scientific and Cultural Organization, p. 5. Available at https://unfccc.int/sites/default/files/resource/Guide_Integrating%20ACE%20into%20NDCs.pdf.

17. Paas and Goodman (2016), p. 4.

18. United Nations (2007) *United Nations Declaration on the Rights of Indigenous Peoples* [Online]. Available at https://www.un.org/development/desa/Indigenouspeoples/declaration-on-the-rights-of-Indigenous-peoples.html.

19. See Appendix B.

20. See Appendix A.

21. See Appendix B.

22. United Nations Climate Change (2018) *2018 Talanoa Dialogue Platform* [Online]. Available at https://unfccc.int/process-and-meetings/the-paris-agreement/the-paris-agreement/2018-talanoa-dialogue-platform.

23. United Nations Education Sector (2020), p. 3.

24. "Climate education, communication, and outreach" is an expression used by the UNFCCC to encompass all aspects of ACE. See, for example, Climate Education, Communication and Outreach Stakeholders Community (2020) [Online]. Available at www.climateecos.org.

25. Paas and Goodman (2016), p. 6.

26. See, for example: University of Illinois (2020) *Center for Culturally Responsive Evaluation and Assessment* [Online]. Available at https://crea.education.illinois.edu. Methodologies may also include further survey work, such as the *Global Warming's Six Americas* series, as well as

landscape analysis and other approaches.

27. Vandello, J. A., Cohen, D. (1999) 'Patterns of individualism and collectivism across the United States', *Journal of Personality and Social Psychology*, vol. 77, no. 2, pp. 279–2.

28. See the Yale University/George Mason University (n.d.) *Global Warming's Six Americas* series [Online]. Available at https://climatecommunication.yale.edu/about/projects/global-warmings-six-americas/.

29. United States Global Research Program (2009) *Climate Literacy: The Essential Principles of Climate Science* [Online]. Available at: https://www.climate.gov/teaching/essential-principles-climate-literacy/essential-principles-climate-literacy. See also: Climate Literacy and Energy Awareness Network [Online]. Available at https://cleanet.org/clean/literacy/index.html.

30. Stapleton, S. R. (2019) 'A case for climate justice education: American youth connecting to intergenerational climate injustice in Bangladesh', *Environmental Education Research*, vol. 25, no. 5, pp. 732–50. See also: National Science Teaching Association (2020) 'Social justice-centered science teaching and learning', 26 May [Online]. Available at https://www.nsta.org/blog/social-justice-science-classroom.

31. National Research Council (2012) *A Framework for K-12 Science Education: Practices, Crosscutting Concepts, and Core Ideas* [Online]. Washington, DC: National Academies Press. Available at https://www.nap.edu/catalog/13165/a-framework-for-k-12-science-education-practices-crosscutting-concepts.

32. NGSS Lead States (2013) *Next Generation Science Standards: For States, By States.* Washington, DC: National Academies Press. Available at https://www.nextgenscience.org.

33. See for example: National Association for the Advancement of Colored People (2020) *Environmental and Climate Justice Program* [Online]. Available at https://www.naacp.org/

environmental-climate-justice-about/. See also: Climate Justice Alliance (n.d.) *Just Transition: A Framework for Change* [Online]. Available at https://climatejusticealliance.org/just-transition/. See also: Indigenous Environmental Network (2020) [Online]. Available at https://www.ienearth.org/. See also: Bullard, R. D. (Ed.) (1963) *Confronting Environmental Racism: Voices from the Grassroots*. Cambridge, MA: South End Press. See also: Bullard, R. D., Gardezi, M., Chennault, C., Dankbar, H. (2016) 'Climate change and environmental justice: A conversation with Dr. Robert Bullard', *Journal of Critical Thought and Praxis*, vol. 5, no. 2 [Online]. Available at https://doi.org/10.31274/jctp-180810-61. See also: Bullard, R. D., Warren, R. C., Johnson, G. S. (2005) *The Quest for Environmental Justice: Human Rights and the Politics of Pollution*. San Francisco, CA: Sierra Club Books.

34. See, for example: Climate Generation (2020) [Online]. Available at https://www.climategen.org/. See also: Climate Literacy and Energy Awareness Network (2020) [Online]. Available at https://cleanet.org/index.html.

35. Kluttz, J. and Walter, P. (2018) 'Conceptualizing learning in the climate justice movement', *Adult Education Quarterly*, vol. 68, no. 22, pp. 91–107.

36. Worland, J. (2019).

37. Brondolo, E., Libretti, M., Rivera, L., Walsemann, K. M. (2012) 'Racism and social capital: The implications for social and physical well-being', *Journal of Social Issues*, vol. 68, no. 2, pp. 358–84.

38. Horowitz, J. M., Igielnik, R., Kochhar, R. (2020) 'Trends in income and wealth inequality', *Social & Demographic Trends*, Pew Research Center, 9 January [Online]. Available at https://www.pewsocialtrends.org/2020/01/09/trends-in-income-and-wealth-inequality/.

39. For clarification of terms, see Racial Equity Tools (2020) *Glossary* [Online]. Available at https://www.racialequitytools.

org/glossary.

40. See Racial Equity Tools (2020).

41. Goldberg, M., et al. (2020).

42. Kotcher, J., Maibach, E., Montoro, M., Hassol, S. J. (2018) 'How Americans respond to information about global warming's health impacts: Evidence from a national survey experiment', *American Geophysical Union Fall Meeting*, 12 September [Online]. Available at https://doi.org/10.1029/2018GH000154.

43. Kotcher, J., Maibach, E., Rosenthal, S., Gustafson, A., Leiserowitz, L. (2020) 'Americans increasingly understand that climate change harms human health', *Climate Notes*, 15 June [Online]. George Mason University Center for Climate Change Communication. Available at https://www.climatechangecommunication.org/all/americans-increasingly-understand-that-climate-change-harms-human-health/.

44. Myers, T., Maibach, E. W., Placky, B. W., Henry, K. L., Slater, M. D., Seitter, K. L. (2020) 'Impact of the Climate Matters program on public understanding of climate change', *Weather, Climate, and Society*, vol. 12, no. 4, pp. 863–76 [Online]. Available at https://doi.org/10.1175/WCAS-D-20-0026.1.

45. Plutzer, E., McCaffrey, M., Hannah, A. L., Rosenau, J., Berbeco, M., Reid, A. H. (2016) 'Climate confusion among US teachers', *Science*, vol. 351, no. 6274, pp. 664–5 [Online]. Available at https://science.sciencemag.org/content/351/6274/664.

46. See National Center for Science Education [Online]. Available at https://ncse.ngo/.

47. Morrison, D., Annamma, S. A., Jackson, D. D. (Eds.) (2017) *Critical Race Spatial Analysis: Mapping to Understand and Address Educational Inequity*. Sterling, VA: Stylus Publishing.

48. Griffiths, A. (2020) 'If you're not centering justice you're not going to solve the problem', *Climate Xchange*, 29

October [Online]. Available at https://climate-xchange.org/2020/10/29/if-youre-not-centering-justice-youre-not-going-to-solve-the-problem/?mc_cid=56a56eccaa&mc_eid=5a36516057.

49. Lashof, D. (2019) 'US coronavirus response: 3 principles for sustainable economic stimulus', *World Resources Institute*, 20 March [Blog]. Available at https://www.wri.org/blog/2020/03/coronavirus-US-economic-stimulus.

50. *Science News* (2013) 'Big data, for better or worse: 90% of world's data generated over the last two years', *Science Daily*, 22 May [Online]. Available at https://www.sciencedaily.com/releases/2013/05/130522085217.htm.

51. Carr, S. (2020) 'How many ads do we see a day in 2020?', *PPC Project*, 9 April [Blog]. Available at https://ppcprotect.com/how-many-ads-do-we-see-a-day/.

52. Maibach, E., Myers, T., Leiserowitz, A. (2014) 'Climate scientists need to set the record straight: There is a scientific consensus that human-caused climate change is happening', *Advancing Earth and Space Science*, 4 April [Online]. Available at https://agupubs.onlinelibrary.wiley.com/doi/full/10.1002/2013EF000226.

53. See, for example: Oreskes and Conway (2010).

54. See also: National Center for Science Education (2017) *NCSE's counter-Heartland flyers*, 27 April [Online]. Available at https://ncse.ngo/ncses-counter-heartland-flyers.

55. Leiserowitz, et al. (2018).

56. Edelman (2019) *2019 Edelman Trust Barometer Global Report* [Online]. Edelman. Available at https://www.edelman.com/sites/g/files/aatuss191/files/2019-02/2019_Edelman_Trust_Barometer_Global_Report.pdf.

57. Hultman, et al. (2019).

58. Back-casting is an exercise in which people start by describing a desired future and then identify the steps that are needed at various points along the way to create that

future. See Appendix A.

59. Banks, J. A., Au, K. H., Ball, A. F., Bell, P., Gordon, E. W., Gutierrez, K. D., Zhou, M. (2007) *Learning In and Out of School in Diverse Environments: Life-long, Life-wide, Life-deep* [Online]. Seattle, WA: The LIFE Center. Available at http://life-slc.org/docs/Banks_etal-LIFE-Diversity-Report.pdf.

60. See, for example: UNFCCC (2020) *Common Metrics* [Online]. Available at https://unfccc.int/process-and-meetings/transparency-and-reporting/methods-for-climate-change-transparency/common-metrics.

61. Social and emotional learning (referred to as "social-emotional learning" or "SEL") involves attending to the emotions of individuals as part of the learning process, including showing empathy, building relationships, and learning to recognize and manage emotions. See, for example: CASEL (2020) [Online]. Available at https://casel.org/.

62. Fischhoff, B. (2007) 'Nonpersuasive communication about matters of greatest urgency: Climate change', *Environmental Science & Technology*, vol. 41, no. 21, pp. 7204–8 [Online]. Available at https://pubs.acs.org/doi/10.1021/es0726411# (Accessed 18 August 2020), p. 7206.

63. Gould, R. (2011) 'What does it take to market social and behavioral change?', paper presented at Carbon Smarts Conference. Lowell, MA, 20 October.

64. United Nations Education Sector (2020), p. 4.

65. See also North American Association for Environmental Education (2017) *Guidelines for Excellence: Community Engagement* [Online]. Available at https://cdn.naaee.org/sites/default/files/eepro/resource/files/community_engagement_-_guidelines_for_excellence_0.pdf.

66. Yankelovich, D. (1999) *The Magic of Dialogue*. New York, NY: Touchstone, p. 17.

67. Bang, M., Faber, L., Gurneau, J., Marin, A., Soto, C. (2016)

'Community-based design research: Learning across generations and strategic transformations of institutional relations toward axiological innovations', *Mind, Culture, and Activity*, vol. 23, no. 1, pp. 28–41.

68. Bryk, A. S., Gomez, L. M., Grunow, A., LeMahieu, P. G. (2015) *Learning to Improve: How America's Schools Can Get Better at Getting Better.* Cambridge, MA: Harvard Education Press. See also: Yeager, D., Bryk, A., Muhich, J., Hausman, H., Morales, L. (2013) *Practical Measurement* [Online]. Palo Alto, CA: Carnegie Foundation for the Advancement of Teaching. Available at https://www.carnegiefoundation. org/wp-content/uploads/2014/09/Practical_Measurement_ Yeager-Bryk1.pdf._

69. "Colonial thinking" encompasses multiple interacting forms of oppression. See, for example: Robinson, M. (2019) *Climate Justice: Hope, Resilience, and the Fight for a Sustainable Future.* New York, NY: Bloomsbury Publishing.

70. Davies, R. and Dart, J. (2005) 'Most significant change: A complexity-aware monitoring approach' [Online]. Available at https://usaidlearninglab.org/library/most-significant-change-complexity-aware-monitoring-approach.

71. Morgan, T. K. K. B., F'Aui, T. N., Bennet, P. (2015) 'Decision support systems: Just about money or more than that?', *E-proceedings of the 36th IAHR World Congress,* The Hague, 28 June – 2 July [Online]. Available at https://www. researchgate.net/publication/280737981_DECISION_ SUPPORT_SYSTEMS_JUST_ABOUT_MONEY_OR_MORE_ THAN_THAT

72. See, for example: Adhikari S. R. (2016) 'Methods of measuring externalities', in Adhikari, S. R., *Economics of Urban Externalities: SpringerBriefs in Economics* [Online]. Singapore: Springer. Available at https://doi.org/10.1007/978-981-10-0545-9_2. Also: measurement of externalities is largely based

on Hardin, G. (1968), 'The tragedy of the commons', *Science*, vol. 162, no. 3859, pp. 1243–8 (13 December).

73. Fischhoff, B. (2007), p. 7206.

74. Fischhoff, B. (2007), p. 7206.

75. Kaplan, S. (2020) 'How America's hottest city will survive climate change', *The Washington Post*, 8 July [Online]. Available at https://www.washingtonpost.com/graphics/2020/climate-solutions/phoenix-climate-change-heat/?no_nav=true&tid=a_classic-iphone&p9w22b2p=b2p22p9w00098.

76. See, for example: Myers, T, Maibach, E. W., Placky, B. W., Henry, K. L., Slater, M. D., Seitter, K. L. (2020) 'Impact of the Climate Matters program on public understanding of climate change', *Weather, Climate, and Society*, vol. 12, no. 4, pp. 863–76 [Online]. American Meteorological Society. Available at https://doi.org/10.1175/WCAS-D-20-0026.1.

77. In this context, "evidence-based" draws on diverse methodologies from social science, decision science, and learning science, particularly the perspectives of BIPOC scholars.

78. United Nations Education Sector (2020), p. 4.

79. Valentino, L. (2019) *Announcing New Programs Manager for Climate Change and Climate Justice*. Portland, OR: Portland Public Schools. Available at https://www.pps.net/cms/lib/OR01913224/Centricity/Domain/4/Programs-Manager_Climate-Change.pdf.

80. Bowman, T. (2016) *Toward Consensus on the Climate Communication Challenge: Report from a Dialogue of Researchers and Practitioners* [Online]. Bowman Change, Inc. Available at https://www.tombowman.com/resources.

81. See examples in State of Washington Office of the Superintendent of Public Instruction (n.d.) *Climate Time: Climate Science Learning* [Online]. Available at www.climetime.org. See also: Governor Phil Murphy (2020) 'First

lady Murphy announces New Jersey will be first state in the nation to incorporate climate change across education guidelines for K-12', *State of New Jersey*, 3 June [Online]. Available at https://nj.gov/governor/news/news/562020/approved/20200603b.shtml.

82. See, for example: North American Association for Environmental Education (n.d.) *Guidelines for Excellence: Best Practice in EE* [Online]. Available at https://naaee.org/our-work/programs/guidelines-excellence.

83. United Nations Education Sector (2020), p. 4.

84. See, for example: C40 Knowledge (2020) *Cities, Coronavirus (COVID-19) and a Green Recovery* [Online]. Available at https://www.c40knowledgehub.org/s/cities-and-coronavirus-covid-19?language=en_US.

85. See, for example: American Society of Environmental Engineers (n.d.) *Committee on Adaptation to a Changing Climate* [Online]. Available at https://www.asce.org/climate-change/committee-on-adaptation-to-a-changing-climate/.

86. See Harding, S. G. (1998) *Is Science Multicultural? Postcolonialisms, Feminisms, and Epistemologies*. Bloomington, IN: Indiana University Press.

87. United Nations Education Sector (2020), p. 4.

88. Webster, R. and Marshall, G. (2019) *The #TalkingClimate Handbook: How to Have Conversations about Climate Change in Your Daily Life* [Online]. Oxford: Climate Outreach. Available at https://climateoutreach.org/resources/how-to-have-a-climate-change-conversation-talking-climate/.

89. Manion, M., Zarakas, C., Wnuck, S., Haskell, J., Belova, A., Cooley, D., Dorn, J., Hoer, M., Mayo, L. (2017) *Analysis of the Public Health Impacts of the Regional Greenhouse Gas Initiative* [Online]. Available at https://www.abtassociates.com/insights/publications/report/analysis-of-the-public-health-impacts-of-the-regional-greenhouse-gas (Accessed 18 August 2020).

90. Maibach, E., et al. (2014).

91. United Nations Education Sector (2020), p. 4.

92. United Nations Education Sector (2020), p. 4.

93. United Nations Education Sector (2020), p. 4.

94. See, for example: United Nations Climate Change (2020) *UN Local Communities and Indigenous Peoples Platform* [Online]. Available at https://unfccc.int/LCIPP.

95. Paas and Goodman (2016), p. 21.

96. Paas and Goodman (2016), p. 21.

97. See, for example: Engage4Climate, *Engage4Climate Toolkit* [Online]. Available at https://www.asce.org/climate-change/committee-on-adaptation-to-a-changing-climate/.

Chapter 5: Commentaries

1. Alana Semuals (2019) 'Why corporations can no longer avoid politics', *Time Magazine*, 21 November [Online]. Available at https://time.com/5735415/woke-culture-political-companies/.

CHANGEMAKERS
BOOKS

Transform your life, transform *our* world. Changemakers Books publishes books for people who seek to become positive, powerful agents of change. These books inform, inspire, and provide practical wisdom and skills to empower us to write the next chapter of humanity's future.

www.changemakers-books.com

The *Resilience* Series

The Resilience Series is a collaborative effort by the authors of Changemakers Books in response to the 2020 coronavirus pandemic. Each concise volume offers expert advice and practical exercises for mastering specific skills and abilities. Our intention is that by strengthening your resilience, you can better survive and even thrive in a time of crisis.
www.resilience-books.com

Adapt and Plan for the New Abnormal – in the COVID-19 Coronavirus Pandemic
Gleb Tsipursky

Aging with Vision, Hope and Courage in a Time of Crisis
John C. Robinson

Connecting with Nature in a Time of Crisis
Melanie Choukas-Bradley

Going Within in a Time of Crisis
P. T. Mistlberger

Grow Stronger in a Time of Crisis
Linda Ferguson

Handling Anxiety in a Time of Crisis
George Hoffman

Navigating Loss in a Time of Crisis
Jules De Vitto

The Life-Saving Skill of Story
Michelle Auerbach

Virtual Teams – Holding the Center When You Can't Meet Face-to-Face
Carlos Valdes-Dapena

Virtually Speaking – Communicating at a Distance
Tim Ward and Teresa Erickson

Current Bestsellers from Changemakers Books

Pro Truth
A Practical Plan for Putting Truth Back into Politics
Gleb Tsipursky and Tim Ward
How can we turn back the tide of post-truth politics, fake news, and misinformation that is damaging our democracy? In the lead up to the 2020 US Presidential Election, Pro Truth provides the answers.

An Antidote to Violence
Evaluating the Evidence
Barry Spivack and Patricia Anne Saunders
It's widely accepted that Transcendental Meditation can create peace for the individual, but can it create peace in society as a whole? And if it can, what could possibly be the mechanism?

Finding Solace at Theodore Roosevelt Island
Melanie Choukas-Bradley
A woman seeks solace on an urban island paradise in Washington D.C. through 2016–17, and the shock of the Trump election.

the bottom
a theopoetic of the streets
Charles Lattimore Howard
An exploration of homelessness fusing theology, jazz-verse and intimate storytelling into a challenging, raw and beautiful tale.

The Soul of Activism
A Spirituality for Social Change
Shmuly Yanklowitz
A unique examination of the power of interfaith spirituality to fuel the fires of progressive activism.

Future Consciousness
The Path to Purposeful Evolution
Thomas Lombardo
An empowering evolutionary vision of wisdom and the human
mind to guide us in creating a positive future.

Preparing for a World that Doesn't Exist – Yet
Rick Smyre and Neil Richardson
This book is about an emerging Second Enlightenment and the
capacities you will need to achieve success in this new, fast-
evolving world.